Sailing and Seamanship

Sailing and Seamanship

ERIC B. HOWELLS B.A.

Headmaster, Melton Constable Secondary Modern School

Illustrated by W. Megoran F.R.S.A.

Edited by

COMMANDER B. W. LUCKE

Head of the Department of Navigation,
Sir Anthony Deane County Secondary School,
Dovercourt, Harwich

Longmans

LONGMANS, GREEN AND CO LTD
48 GROSVENOR STREET, LONDON WI
RAILWAY CRESCENT, CROYDON, VICTORIA, AUSTRALIA
443 LOCKHART ROAD, HONG KONG
PRIVATE MAIL BAG 1036, IKEJA (LAGOS)
44 JALAN AMPANG, KUALA LUMPUR
ACCRA, AUCKLAND, IBADAN, KINGSTON (JAMAICA)
NAIROBI, SALISBURY (RHODESIA)
LONGMANS SOUTHERN AFRICA (PTY) LTD
THIBAULT HOUSE, THIBAULT SQUARE, CAPE TOWN
LONGMANS, GREEN AND CO INC
119 WEST 40TH STREET, NEW YORK 18
LONGMANS, GREEN AND CO
137 BOND STREET, TORONTO 2
ORIENT LONGMANS PRIVATE LTD
CALCUTTA, BOMBAY, MADRAS
DELHI, HYDERABAD, DACCA

Acknowledgment
The publishers are most grateful to the Fibres Division of the
I.C.I. at Harrogate for their generous assistance

Printed and bound in Great Britain
by Jarrold and Sons Ltd, Norwich

INTRODUCTION BY THE EDITOR, COMMANDER B. W. LUCKE

This book has been written for those who like messing about in small boats. I have had the privilege of watching it grow from the first draft to the finished book and I am sure that *Sailing and Seamanship* will appeal to sailing folk of all ages, as well as to those studying the subject in schools and clubs.

'If a thing is worth doing at all, it is worth doing badly', but sailing is much more fun and a great deal safer if it is done well. The more we know about sailing, the greater will be our skill, and the greater our skill the greater our pleasure.

Seamanship is 'All about the sea, all about the man, and all about the ship'. *All* is a big word, but the reader will find that after he has mastered each chapter there are suggestions for further reading and, above all, for things to do, which will increase his practical knowledge and widen his experience.

Sails and sailormen are as full of tradition and history as most things and the influence of the past has not been forgotten in writing about the present. Nevertheless, this book is as modern as the day. Indeed it is more than this, for an Appendix on the Rule of the Road at Sea has been included which gives us a preview of what the law will be in two or three years' time. Lack of space makes it impossible to deal with all the changes which will be taking place, so that only those applying to sailing vessels have been included. When the time comes the new law will be issued as a *Notice to Mariners* and the full details will be available to everyone.

Not only is the author a yachtsman of great experience, but he is also a teacher of sailing. There must be many hundreds of people whose pleasure in sailing rests upon a foundation laid by Eric Howells. He has devoted much of his spare time over many years to teaching youngsters to manage and care for small craft. *Sailing and Seamanship* is the fruit of this long and voluntary service.

Winston Megoran, himself a yachtsman, has translated the author's ideas into pictures and diagrams which are as clear as they are numerous. It is not often that a technical book is so well illustrated as this one, and the use of two colours makes the chapter on The Buoyage System absolutely clear and realistic. The generosity of the I.C.I. Fibres Division at Harrogate has made this possible.

This book will help the reader to understand what he sees afloat and to make fewer mistakes. If in doing so he gets as much enjoyment out of sailing as the Editor has done in his own life, he has many happy days ahead of him.

BOOKS FOR FURTHER READING

*SAILING AND SMALL BOATS FOR BOYS AND GIRLS, *by J. M. Lewis*   *E.U.P. 6/-*
*SAILING, *by Lawrence Sandy*   *1953 Puffin Picture Book 2/6*
*SAILING. KNOW THE GAME SERIES
*THE YOUNG SAILOR, *by Guy Pennant*   *1951 A. & C. Black 10/6*
DINGHY SAILING FOR BOYS AND GIRLS, *by Sir G. Nightingale*   *Adlard Coles*
*THE BOSUN BOOKS, *various authors*   *Adlard Coles*
DINGHY OWNERSHIP, *by Sir G. Nightingale*   *1956 Adlard Coles 15/-*
SAILING, *by Peter Heaton*   *1955 Penguin*
OFFSHORE, *by John Illingworth*   *1949 Ross 63/-*
HOW TO SAIL, *by John Fisher*   *1953 Eyre & Spottiswoode 12/6*
SAILING BOATS, *by Uffa Fox*   *Newnes*
NEW SMALL BOAT SAILING, *by John Fisher*   *Adlard Coles*
MANUAL OF SEAMANSHIP, Vol. I   *1951 H.M.S.O. 8/6*
MANUAL OF SEAMANSHIP, Vol. II   *1951 H.M.S.O. 8/6*
A SEAMAN'S POCKET BOOK   *1943 H.M.S.O.*
SEA SCOUT HANDBOOK   *Boy Scouts Association 8/6*
NAVIGATION GUIDE FOR SECONDARY EDUCATION, *by Macsween*
    1952 Brown, Son & Ferguson 12/6
A FIRST BOOK OF NAVIGATION, *by L. L. Johnson*   *1948 Macmillan 2/6*
CELESTIAL NAVIGATION FOR YACHTSMEN, *by Mary Blewitt 1950 Yachting World 5/-*
ELEMENTARY MARINE NAVIGATION, *by Walling & Hill*   *Cambridge University Press*
BENDS, HITCHES, KNOTS AND SPLICES, *by John Irving*   *1952 Seeley Services 6/-*
DISCOVERING SAILING SHIPS, *by C. R. France*   *1955 U.L.P. 8/6*
SAILING SHIPS, *by A. White*   *1951 Puffin Picture Book 2/6*
SHIPS AND MEN, *by Bassett Lowke and Holland*   *Harrap*
RACING DINGHY HANDLING, *by Ian Procter*   *1948 Adlard Coles 15/-*
BETTER SMALL BOAT HANDLING, *by John Fisher*   *1955 Adlard Coles 15/-*
FASTER SAILING, *by R. N. Bavier*   *1956 Nicholas Kaye 21/-*
SAILING WIND AND CURRENT, *by Ian Procter*   *1956 Adlard Coles 16/-*
THE DINGHY YEAR BOOK, 1958–1961   *Adlard Coles*
RACING DINGHY MAINTENANCE, *by Ian Procter*   *1956 Adlard Coles 15/-*
AMATEUR BOAT BUILDING, *by Michael Verney*   *1958 10/6*
*FROM CORACLES TO CUNARDERS, *by L. Snellgrove*   *Longmans 9/6*
*THE WONDER BOOK OF THE SEASHORE, *by Marie Neurath*   *1954 Max Parrish 7/6*
THE ADVENTURE OF WHALING, *by Frank Crisp*   *1954 Macmillan 6/6*
*BOAT MODELLING, *by V. Smeed*   *Model Aero Press, Watford*
YACHT RACING RULES SIMPLIFIED, *by H. Somerville*   *1956 Adlard Coles 3/6*
MODEL BOAT CONSTRUCTION, *by H. Adam*   *1952 Percival Marshall 42/-*

* More suitable for younger readers.

MAGAZINES
Light Craft
Yachts and Yachting
Yachting Monthly
Yachting World
Motor Boat and Yachting

CONTENTS

1. Finding Your Way About a Boat

Positions relating to boats

Before going afloat to look at the boats in the harbour, here are some of the terms that describe positions inside and outside boats and the directions in which boats move.

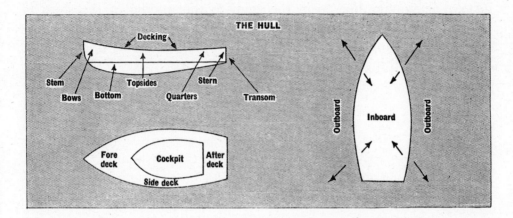

Summary of terms mentioned in the diagrams above

(1) The HULL is the body of the boat. The names given to the parts of its surface are:

The DECKS—the surfaces that face upwards and are nearly horizontal.

TOPSIDES—the sides above the water-line.

BOTTOM—the sides below the water-line that go under the boat and meet at the keel.

BOWS—the curved sides forward that meet at the STEM.

QUARTERS—the sides which curve in gently aft to the STERN or TRANSOM.

STEM—where the topsides meet right forward.

STERN—where the topsides meet right aft.

TRANSOM—a flat as opposed to a pointed stern.

(2) Anything outside the hull is described as OUTBOARD and anything inside as INBOARD.

1

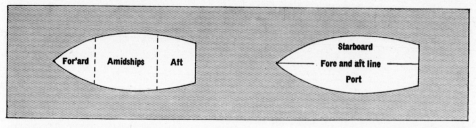

(3) Inside the hull there are three main divisions of the space—
FOR'ARD or FOREPART, AMIDSHIPS, and AFT or AFTERPART,
also known as STERNSHEETS.

(4) An imaginary line from the stem to the middle of the stern is
known as the centre FORE-AND-AFT LINE.

(5) When looking forward everything to the left of this line is PORT
and everything to the right is STARBOARD.

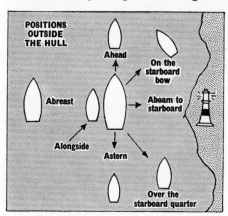

(6) The position of objects outside
the hull is described as being
on port and starboard, in combination with other terms, e.g.
over the starboard bow.

ABEAM—at right angles to the
imaginary fore and aft line of
the hull.

ALONGSIDE—side by side and
touching the hull.

ABREAST—level with the hull
but not touching it.

(7) Terms which describe the movement of the boat.

UNDER WAY—when the boat is not secured to a mooring or not
at anchor.

MAKING WAY or HAS WAY ON—when the boat is actually
moving through the water.

ADRIFT—a boat that has broken away from her mooring or
anchor and has no means of propelling herself.

STEERAGE WAY—when a boat has enough movement through
the water to make her rudder effective.

To GO AHEAD—is to make HEADWAY or move forwards.

To MOVE ASTERN—is to make STERNWAY or move backwards.

BROADSIDE ON—is to move sideways.

LEEWAY—the movement of a boat which is involuntarily blown
sideways by the wind when going ahead or astern.

2. The Harbour and Dinghy Park–
Anchoring and Moorings

The harbour and dinghy park

Boats that are IN COMMISSION, that is, ready for use, are kept in an ANCHORAGE either on MOORINGS or AT ANCHOR. The anchorage is usually in a HARBOUR sheltered from strong winds and rough seas. There is always a channel called a FAIRWAY in the harbour which is kept clear for the passage of boats to and from the harbour and a JETTY or SLIPWAY which runs out from the shore.

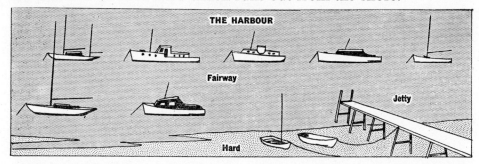

Some small boats are not kept afloat but in a DINGHY PARK, which is somewhat like a car park. A dinghy park should be close to the water. It should have a good entrance and a clear path to the sea with no overhead wires to get caught up with masts. Boats are moved on a LAUNCHING TROLLEY from the dinghy park to the water.

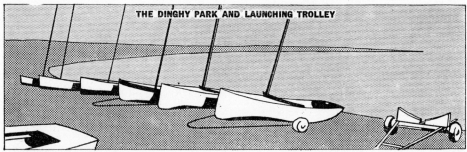

They are safe in a dinghy park in any weather. Many of the small, light sailing dinghies in use today are not designed to be left afloat permanently. Boats are sometimes drawn up on a HARD which is either a natural formation of sand and gravel or a man-made strip of foreshore built up over the mud. Hards are in common use as landing places for boats.

3

Anchors and anchoring

In the harbour there will be some boats stationed clear of one another and equally spaced in orderly lines. These boats are on moorings.

Other boats will be lying in a less orderly fashion and may be FOULING one another. These boats are at anchor.

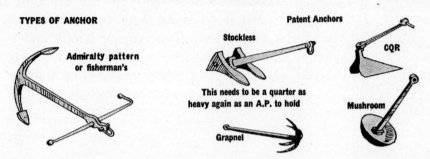

TYPES OF ANCHOR

Patent Anchors

Admiralty pattern or fisherman's

Stockless

CQR

This needs to be a quarter as heavy again as an A.P. to hold

Mushroom

Grapnel

There are many types of anchor and they are designed to do a particular job and to suit different kinds of sea-bed.

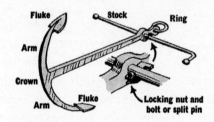

PARTS OF THE ADMIRALTY PATTERN ANCHOR

Fluke   Stock   Ring

Arm

Crown

Arm   Fluke

Locking nut and bolt or split pin

The most common type of anchor is the ADMIRALTY PATTERN or FISHERMAN'S ANCHOR which is probably the best for general use. An anchor has a crown, arms, flukes, shank, stock and ring to which the anchor chain or rope is made fast.

How the anchor works

The boat pulls on the chain or rope and as the anchor begins to move along the fluke bites into the sea-bed and the anchor holds the boat against wind and tide. The stock prevents the anchor from toppling over on its side and becoming ineffective.

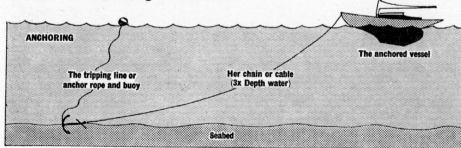

ANCHORING

The tripping line or anchor rope and buoy

Her chain or cable (3x Depth water)

The anchored vessel

Seabed

The sea-bed or bottom is often referred to as the HOLDING GROUND into which the anchor bites and holds. Hard mud is best for anchoring, soft mud and sand is fairly good and shingle and rock is bad.

The size of the anchor to be used is important. For small boats of under 20 feet in length, 1 lb. of Admiralty Pattern anchor is advisable for every foot of boat length. Certain patent anchors like a CQR have better holding power and may be much smaller and lighter.

The length of an anchor chain or rope should be at least three times the depth of water in which the boat is anchored plus the amount of the rise of the tide. Except in dinghies which use coir rope or hemp about 3 inches in circumference, chain is always safer because it helps to weigh down the anchor.

Using the anchor

Before coming to anchor TAKE WAY OFF your boat by letting her slow down against the flow of the tide which acts as a brake. If necessary let her stop. Then lower the anchor until it touches the sea-bed. This is known as CASTING ANCHOR.

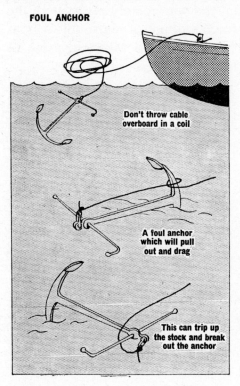

FOUL ANCHOR

Don't throw cable overboard in a coil

A foul anchor which will pull out and drag

This can trip up the stock and break out the anchor

Never throw the rest of the anchor rope overboard in a coil but as the boat moves astern pay it out slowly to avoid fouling the anchor with its own rope. Inside the boat, the anchor rope is made fast to the SAMSON POST or KING POST, or to a strong cleat bolted securely to the main structure of the boat, or to an eyebolt or ring.

Your anchor cable should be marked to show how much has been payed out. Anchors are apt to get foul of telegraph cables and other anchor warps on the sea-bed. When WEIGHING ANCHOR, that is, when getting the anchor up off the sea-bed, it sometimes refuses to come up. TO BREAK OUT THE ANCHOR, that is, to free the flukes

5

THE TRIPPING LINE OR ANCHOR BUOY AND ROPE

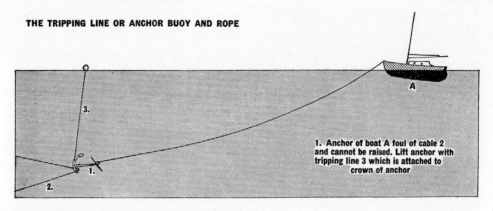

1. Anchor of boat A foul of cable 2 and cannot be raised. Lift anchor with tripping line 3 which is attached to crown of anchor

from the holding ground, either a TRIPPING LINE or anchor buoy and rope is often attached near the crown before the anchor is put down. The anchor is freed by pulling on these ropes which are made of much smaller line than the main anchor cable.

Moorings

Technically a mooring is a device for securing a boat to the sea-bed which the crew cannot get back on board with the boat's own gear.

The advantage of a mooring is that the boat merely pivots with the change of tide and occupies only a small amount of sea-room. A boat on a single anchor swings about her anchor and takes up a lot of room; a boat moored on two anchors takes up less room.

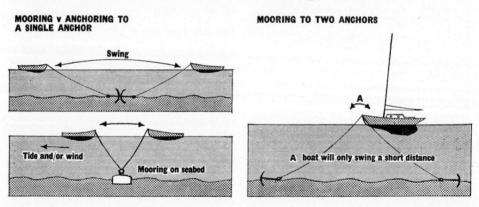

MOORING v ANCHORING TO A SINGLE ANCHOR

Swing

Tide and/or wind

Mooring on seabed

MOORING TO TWO ANCHORS

A boat will only swing a short distance

Permanent moorings consist of a GROUND CHAIN, RIDING SCOPE, and a short MOORING ROPE AND BUOY. The ground chain is made fast to the sea-bed with extra large and heavy anchors, sometimes with one arm and fluke sawn off or with mudweights such as concrete blocks sometimes referred to as SINKERS.

6

A TROT OF MOORINGS

1. Ground chain
2. Heavy anchor with one arm bent over
3. Heavy sinker
4. Mooring rope or pennant and buoy
5. Riding scope

Moorings set out in the harbour with room for several boats on the ground chain, each on her own riding scope, are often known as a TROT.

Moorings may be put down and organized by harbour commissioners and are under the control of the harbourmaster. Sometimes a boatyard performs a similar service and often the work is organized by a sailing club. Owners of boats may put down their own private moorings if they are allowed to do so.

Lines of moorings are selected according to local conditions such as the direction of the prevailing winds and tides, the shelter available, the depth of water and the kind of sea-bed. The object is to keep boats safe from storms and clear of one another.

Temporary moorings

A temporary mooring can be made by using two anchors some distance from one another and in a line with the prevailing wind and tide. The amount of rope or chain paid out is the same as for a single anchor. The second anchor may be carried out astern in a dinghy when the boat is lying comfortably to her main or 'best bower' anchor. The second anchor warp is not made fast aft but led in through the same fairlead as the first anchor warp so that the boat is free to pivot about this point with the wind and tide.

The disadvantages of using the two-anchor type of mooring is that:
  (i) a strong wind may blow up at right angles to the line of the anchors and as a result they may drag;
  (ii) as the boat swings round and round to the wind and tide she will twist her two cables together and get a thoroughly 'foul hawse' which may be difficult to clear.

A true mooring is more permanent.

7

Picking up a mooring

A small buoy that is taken aboard—lean over from the topsides or foredeck forward and pick it up. Haul the rope aboard (or it may be chain) and secure inboard. If the boat has high sides and you cannot reach the buoy by hand use a boat-hook and pick up the rope underneath the buoy, not any ring or loop that may be on it. Lay the rope or chain in the anchor fairlead.

If it is a large mooring buoy or flat that is not picked up, secure a warp aboard and pass it through the eye or ring on the buoy and then take back aboard and make fast.

Letting go moorings

(1) If you are leaving a dinghy on the mooring secure it to the mooring buoy.

(2) If the buoy is aboard release the warp and throw the buoy overboard.

(3) If you are made fast to a mooring buoy which is not aboard slip your warp.

Making fast to a jetty or river bank

A river bank

A river is generally narrow and room to manoeuvre is restricted. Boats streaming off the bank would take up too much room so they are made fast *fore and aft* and *fenders* are used to protect the sides of the boat from the bank.

A jetty

Boats are moored less frequently fore and aft along a jetty but are streamed off by a for'ard warp. They stream off the jetty generally to the tide but sometimes to the wind. Streaming off saves room along the jetty. Sometimes, especially in lake moorings, boats are moored head to jetty and stern to buoys.

Looking at boats in a harbour

It is worth having a look round the harbour. You will see motor-boats driven by engines which seamen often call power boats. Some of these power boats, especially those that go fishing, carry one sail known as a STEADYING SAIL which is used to reduce the boat's roll in broken water.

Some boats rely entirely on their sails and have no engines. Others are designed to sail well in a good breeze but to do without sail when the wind is light. Then they use engines only. They are known as 50/50 SAILORS or MOTOR SAILORS. Sometimes an engine is fitted to a sailing-boat to help her navigate in restricted and narrow channels and in harbours that are crowded. This is known as an AUXILIARY ENGINE. Some small boats rely on help from an OUTBOARD MOTOR while most small boat sailors choose to sail with no engines at all.

Small sailing boats vary very much according to their amount of decking, from the completely OPEN BOAT to the FULLY DECKED cabin yacht. In between there are boats with only a fore-deck and HALF DECKERS with a fore-deck, side-decks, after-deck and cockpit for helmsman and crew.

The variety of rigs and rigging, sails and the shape and build of these boats is described in later chapters.

Going aboard a sailing cruiser

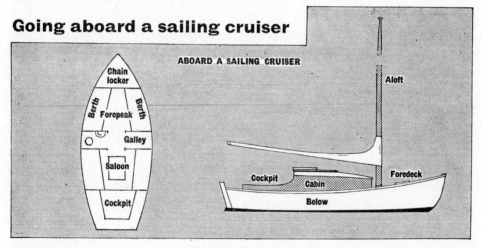

ABOARD A SAILING CRUISER

When the dinghy is made fast go aboard. You step up on deck and then down into the cockpit. One member of the crew has gone FOR'ARD to work and another has gone ALOFT to attend to some rigging that is FOUL. You are invited to go BELOW and you do so through a HATCHWAY and then down a LADDER. You are then in the SALOON which also has two SETTEE BERTHS. You pass for'ard from the saloon through the GALLEY into the FOREPEAK where there are two more berths. Right for'ard in the forepeak is the CHAIN LOCKER. All these terms which describe place and position are important and may be followed quite clearly in the accompanying diagram.

9

Classification of boats in general

Before studying boats in detail, consider (1) how they are driven, and (2) the job they do.

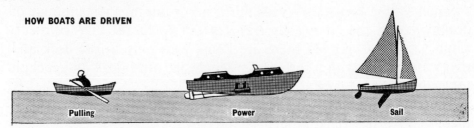

HOW BOATS ARE DRIVEN

Pulling · Power · Sail

How boats are driven

There are three ways in which boats move through the water. They are pulled by oars, driven by propellers or driven by the wind. Boats pulled by oars are known as PULLING BOATS or ROWING BOATS. Boats driven by propellers are called POWER CRAFT and their propellers are turned by engines. The Ministry of Transport often refer to power craft as being under steam. Boats driven by the wind are called SAILING BOATS.

Except for small craft like canoes and punts built for local conditions, all boats belong to one of these three classes: PULLING BOATS, POWER CRAFT or SAILING BOATS.

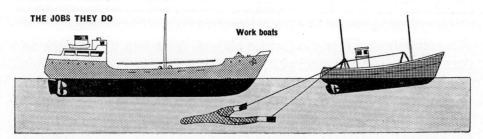

THE JOBS THEY DO

Work boats

The jobs they do

Boats are used either for work or for pleasure. Some WORK BOATS carry cargoes, some carry passengers or both passengers and cargoes and some are engaged in fishing. In addition there are work boats which provide a service—lifeboats, fishery protection vessels, pilot

10

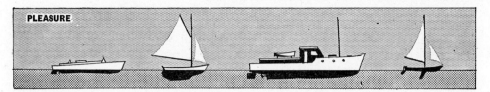

boats and others. Most work boats today are power vessels and very few are still under sail. Special types of work boat built for their particular job include oil tankers, colliers, dredgers, refrigeration ships and ferry boats.

Today the majority of sailing boats are PLEASURE BOATS for cruising, racing and pottering in estuaries, creeks and rivers. Many pleasure boats are power craft.

Classification of sailing boats by rig

To talk about rig it is necessary to know certain technical terms:

Rig

A term which describes the shape and number of sails a boat carries; how and where she carries them. Rig includes masts and spars as well as the sails they support.

The term INBOARD RIG means that there is no sail extending for'ard of the stem and that the boom does not extend aft of the stern. In other words, the sails are all inboard.

The way in which sailing ships today are rigged and the names used to describe rig nearly all come from the old square-rigged sailing ships.

Masts

Long poles of timber or metal tube placed upright in a boat to support sails and spars. Masts are STEPPED into position and named according to their position and length.

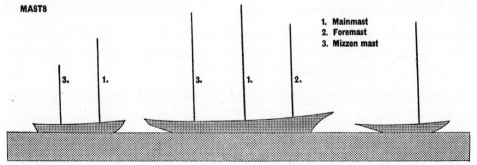

1. Mainmast
2. Foremast
3. Mizzen mast

MAST IN TWO PARTS

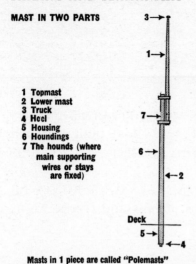

3→

1→

1 Topmast
2 Lower mast
3 Truck
4 Heel
5 Housing
6 Houndings
7 The hounds (where
    main supporting
    wires or stays
    are fixed)

7→

6→

←2

Deck

5→
←4

Masts in 1 piece are called "Polemasts"

They are sometimes made in more than one piece and their various parts have special names.

Spars

Poles which help masts to support sails aloft. Spars include YARDS, GAFFS, SPRITS and BOOMS.

Yard. The original square rig crossed a mast athwartship as shown on p. 13. Today yards extend in the fore and aft line of the boat and hold aloft the head of a four-sided sail.

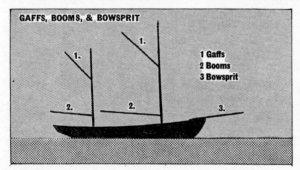

GAFFS, BOOMS, & BOWSPRIT

1.   1.

1 Gaffs
2 Booms
3 Bowsprit

2.   2.   3.

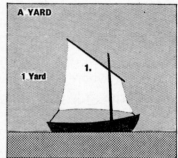

A YARD

1.

1 Yard

Gaff. A spar extending aft and upwards from a mast at an angle of from about 60 degrees to nearly upright; supports the head of a four-sided sail. The lower end next to the mast is fitted with jaws to allow it to move sideways around the mast.

Sprit. A spar which supports a four-sided sail diagonally.

A SPRIT

1 Sprit or Spreet
(hence Spritsail)

1.

Boom. A spar used to secure and extend the bottom edge of a sail.

Bowsprit. A spar extending forward of the bow in the fore and aft line of the boat at deck level to carry forestays and the sails they support.

Bumkin. A short bowsprit of great strength and therefore generally made of iron. Origin *boomkin*. Used to be common on dinghies for'ard. Now rarely found except aft where it serves the purpose of supporting a backstay.

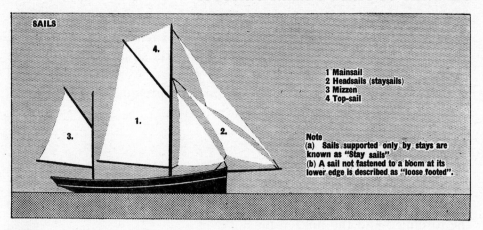

Sails

Known as MAINSAILS, HEADSAILS, MIZZENS or TOPSAILS, according to the position they occupy. They are BENT, that is, fastened and secured, to spars.

Stays

Wires or ropes running from positions on the mast down to the hull. They help to hold the mast upright.

Difference between square-rig and fore-and-aft rig

The FORE-AND-AFT RIG is shown by the line AB in the illustration below. A SQUARE-RIG boat carries sails approximately at right angles to this fore and aft line, that is, athwartship.

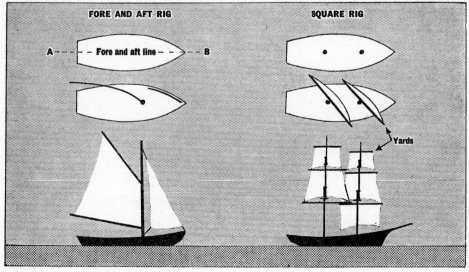

Square-rig

Each sail is bent to a yard. Several sails and their yards are attached to each mast. The sail is four-sided and nearly square in shape. The square rig is an old type of rig now rarely used, except in the topsail of certain types of schooner. It is from the old square-rigged vessels that one meaning of the word SHIP is derived.

Ships

The term SHIP is a fairly common one but it has a special technical meaning. A ship has three masts and is square-rigged on all masts. The middle mast is the tallest and is the mainmast. The other two are the foremast and the mizzen-mast.

A ship is very rarely seen today as few square-rigged vessels are still afloat but it is interesting to record this special meaning of the word ship.

The origin of the word ship is much earlier than square-rigged vessels but the word has been used in this specialized sense for many hundreds of years.

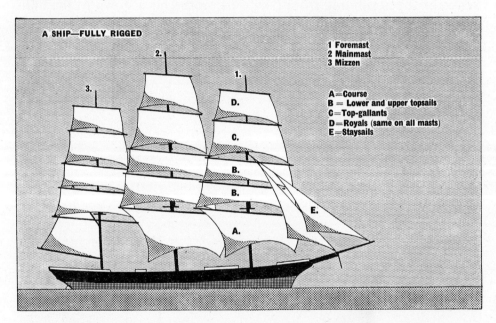

A SHIP—FULLY RIGGED

1 Foremast
2 Mainmast
3 Mizzen

A = Course
B = Lower and upper topsails
C = Top-gallants
D = Royals (same on all masts)
E = Staysails

Sailing boats today are fore-and-aft rigged, identified by
    (1) Shape of the mainsail;
    (2) Number of headsails;
    (3) Number of masts and the position of the shorter mast.

14

(1) Shape of the mainsail:
There are three common kinds of mainsail named by their shape—GAFF, GUN-
TER and BERMUDAN, and they were
developed in that order.

Gaff

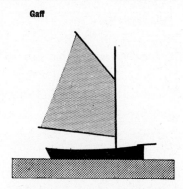

A GAFF mainsail is four-sided and is bent
on to a gaff to hold it up.

Gunter

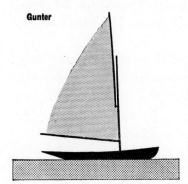

The GUNTER mainsail represents a stage
in development from the older type of
gaff mainsail to the Bermudan mainsail.
The gunter mainsail is bent to a gaff
which can be hoisted close up to the mast.
The set of the sail then resembles a
Bermudan mainsail and it is described as
'high peaked'.

Bermudan

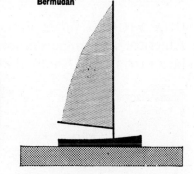

A BERMUDAN mainsail is triangular or
three-sided. It is sometimes called 'A leg
of mutton sail'. Size for size it has a much
taller mast than a gaff mainsail. It does
not need to be attached to a gaff or yard.

The aspect ratio of a mainsail is the ratio of the height of the sail
along the mast to its length along the boom. A Bermudan mainsail can be high or low aspect ratio. High aspect ratio is the more
modern development and the two types look quite different on the
water.

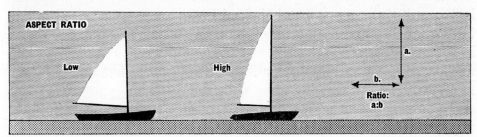

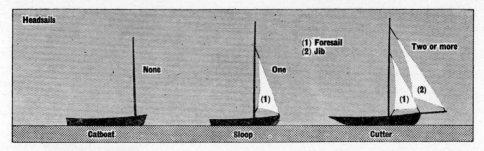

(2) Number of headsails. Boats with one mast and mainsail:
UNA RIGGED CATBOATS . . . no headsail. SLOOPS . . . one headsail.
CUTTERS . . . two or more headsails.

UNA RIGGED boats are often called CATBOATS, particularly in America. The single sail may be gaff, gunter or Bermudan, or it may be a LUGSAIL. Usually the mast will be stepped well forward.

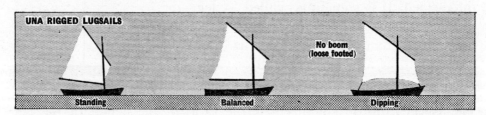

Lugsails are held aloft by a yard and there are three kinds—the STANDING LUG, the BALANCED LUG and the DIPPING LUG. These names help to explain the difference between them.

The standing lug has a yard and generally a boom. Very little sail is forward of the mast. The balanced lug also has a yard and boom but a good deal more sail is forward of the mast. It acts like a headsail in balancing the area aft of the mast. The dipping lug has a yard but no boom. The bottom edge or foot of the sail is said to be LOOSE FOOTED. The dipping lug is so called because the yard has to be dipped and sometimes lowered when moving the sail across from one side of the boat to the other.

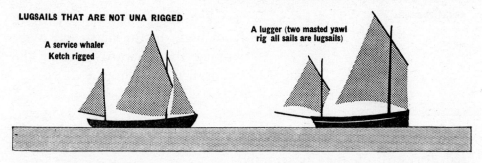

LUGSAILS THAT ARE NOT UNA RIGGED

A service whaler
Ketch rigged

A lugger (two masted yawl
rig all sails are lugsails)

Not all lugsail boats are una rigged. Many Service craft—whalers, cutters, and gigs—use lugsails but are rigged as sloops or ketches. The term cutter as used here describes a type of Service sailing-boat and is different from the meaning used earlier in this chapter. A Service cutter is sloop rigged. Many older coastal fishing vessels also have lugsails but are not una rigged.

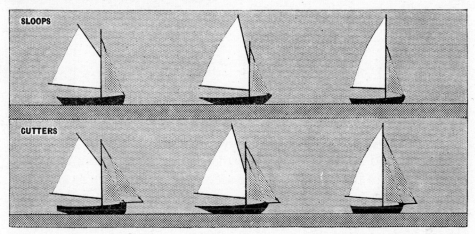

SLOOPS

CUTTERS

A SLOOP has one mast, a mainsail and one headsail. A CUTTER has one mast, a mainsail and two or more headsails. Sloops and cutters are described as gaff, gunter or Bermudan according to the shape of their mainsails.

HEADSAIL is the term used for sails forward of the mast. They are usually supported by being attached to stays and for this reason are sometimes known as STAYSAILS.

Headsails are given different names according to their position. The headsail immediately in front of the main mast is known as the FORESAIL. All sails which are hoisted forward of the foresail are known as JIBS such as the jib topsail otherwise called the flying jib. This is right forward and high on the for'ard stay.

17

GENOA FORESAIL

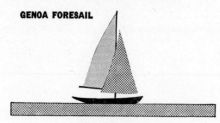

A very large headsail reaching from high up the mast and overlapping the forward part of the mainsail is known as a GENOA.

SPINNAKER

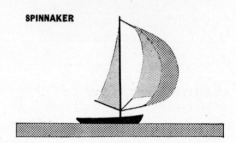

The SPINNAKER is a special sail used forward of the mast only when the wind is blowing from aft. It is a substitute for the foresail under this particular condition.

(3) Number of masts and the position of the shorter mast.

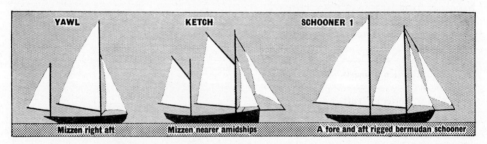

Boats with two masts are either YAWLS, KETCHES or SCHOONERS.

In yawls and ketches the second mast is aft of the mainmast and it is the shorter of the two masts. The second mast is known as a mizzen-mast. It carries a mizzen-sail. In a yawl the mizzen-mast is placed right aft of the boat near or aft of the rudder. In a ketch the mizzen-mast is for'ard of the rudder and placed nearer amidships.

In schooners the additional mast is forward of the mainmast. It is the shorter and is known as the foremast. All sails forward of the mainmast are headsails.

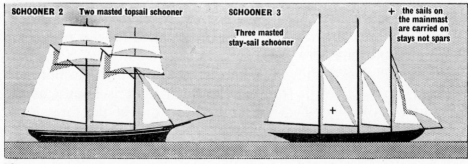

Most schooners today are two-masted. A schooner may have more than two masts and there are still three-masted schooners afloat. The mast aft is called the mizzen if it is shorter than the mainmast.

Schooners carry gaff, gunter or Bermudan mainsails. Schooners with square sails up aloft are known as TOPSAIL SCHOONERS. They are relics of the days of square rig although nowadays they are rigged fore and aft.

Summary: how to identify fore and aft rig

Masts	Headsails	Name	Mainsail	Full name
One	None One Two or more	CATBOAT SLOOP CUTTER	May be GAFF GUNTER BERMUDAN LUGSAIL	e.g. *(a)* a Bermudan sloop *(b)* a gaff cutter
	Position of masts	**Name**	**Mainsail**	**Full name**
Two	Shorter mast aft of mainmast Shorter mast for'ard of mainmast	YAWL (second mast right aft) KETCH (Second mast nearer amidships) SCHOONER	May vary as above	e.g. *(a)* a gaff yawl *(b)* a gaff ketch *(c)* a Bermudan schooner N.B. Topsail and staysail schooner are special names giving further details of rig

The last stronghold of sail

The Thames sailing barges represent 'the last stronghold of sail' among the work boats of the British Isles. They are interesting because they have an unusual rig. They are yawl-rigged, that is, they have a mizzen-mast and sail placed right aft. The mainsail is four-sided and loose-footed because it has no gaff, no yard, and no boom. It is held aloft by a hefty spar running diagonally across it. This spar is a sprit and the mainsail is called a spritsail.

At one time some Thames barges were equipped with bowsprits on which they carried a second headsail.

19

When fully rigged they also carried a topsail between the topmast and the upper edge of the mainsail and a mizzen-mast and sail right aft, as shown below.

Few fully rigged barges now serve as work boats. Many have been reduced to a mainsail and one headsail and are generally fitted with an auxiliary engine, but those converted to pleasure boats as sailing-yachts have often been restored to their original rig.

Fully rigged, the spritsail barges were very manoeuvrable, had a good turn of speed and were excellent load carriers. They were often handled in all sorts of dirty weather off the east coast of England by no more than a crew of two men.

The few remaining work boats carry grain, straw, timber, coal, sand and ballast mainly in the Thames estuary.

4. The Hull

You may not be building your own boat but it is important to know about boat construction to be able to understand the language of the boat-builder and to have a general idea of how a boat is likely to behave when sailing.

Without some knowledge of the technical terms applied to the hull, it would be difficult to understand a typical advertisement for a boat like this:

FOR SALE.
Bermudan sloop. Clinker-built half-decker, straight stem and transom stern, fitted with drop keel.

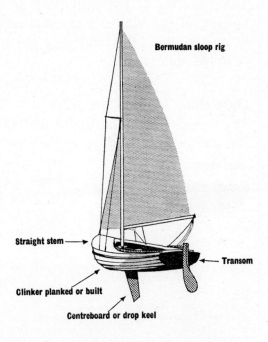

An intelligent discussion with the boatyard on her 'seaworthiness' and performance would be difficult.

Although you will not know exactly how a boat will behave until you sail her, you can get some idea from the construction and shape of her hull to be able to tell whether she was built for inland waters, estuary sailing, or the open sea.

In the main, the language or technical terms which describe the hull refer to:

The main parts of a hull, illustrated in Chapter 1.

The principal forms of construction.

Different materials used for building and how they are used.

Hull performance: (1) shape, (2) measurements.

21

The principal forms of construction

There are two main forms of hull construction. ROUND BILGE and HARD CHINE.

Hulls are built in one of these two forms of construction whether the material is wood, metal or fibreglass.

Round bilge

The topsides of the hull turn into the bottom of the hull in a smooth curve to form a round bilge and give the hull a rounded appearance.

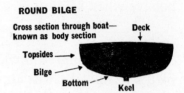

Hard chine

The topsides of the hull and the bottom of the hull each have a flat surface and they form an angle where they join. The line running fore

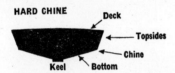

and aft along the side of the hull at the angle formed is the CHINE. This method of construction is HARD CHINE, sometimes referred to as V BOTTOM.

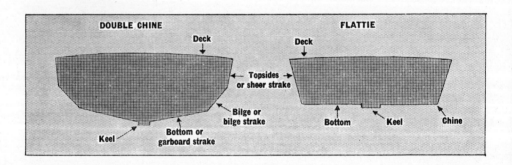

Hulls which have two chines on each side are DOUBLE CHINE and with more than two chines, MULTIPLE CHINE.

Double-chine construction, previously used in larger craft, is now used frequently in building small boats.

There is also a simple form of hard chine hull known as the FLATTIE which is used for rowing dinghies and river barges. It has a flat bottom in cross-section.

Different materials used for building and how they are used

Wood

CLINKER or CLENCH BUILDING is used for small boats of under 30 feet. Although some hard chine boats are CLINKER-BUILT this method is more commonly used for round bilge.

In round bilge boats the hull is built up of planks of wood which are shaped to produce a curved hull. In a 14-foot boat there are about twelve planks to each side and each plank is about 6 inches wide. The main feature of this method of planking is that the planks overlap.

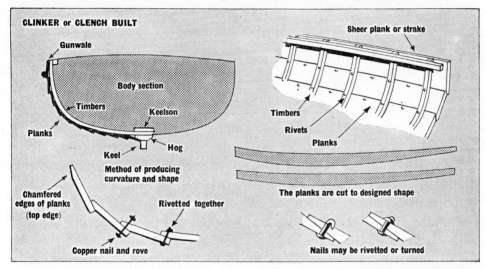

This method of construction is immensely strong. The planks are riveted together with copper boat-nails. To give the hull additional strength the planks are strapped together on the inside of the boat with steamed timbers. The steaming is to soften the timbers and make them more flexible so that they may be bent into position. The timbers run athwartship from one side of the boat to the other and are nailed up and riveted with the planks. In a 14-foot boat the timbers would be set about 6 inches apart and would be about $\frac{7}{8}$ by $\frac{1}{2}$ inch in size.

The planks are made of many timbers including spruce, mahogany, elm, larch, fir, American rock elm, hickory or ash.

PLYWOOD CLINKER-BUILT is a recent development. Planks are cut from plywood and glued together with synthetic waterproof marine glue. This is stronger and less wasteful. There is no need for nailing or strengthening timbers, and cleaning out and maintenance is easier.

23

CARVEL-BUILT is a method of construction for boats with either round bilges or hard chine. It is seldom used for dinghies and more often for boats of 20 feet or over. The difference between this type of building and clinker is that in CARVEL boats the planks do not over-lap but are placed edge to edge. The frames in clinker boats are merely straps to hold the planks together. In carvel boats they are moulded and built up to form until the whole framework is complete. It is then planked over.

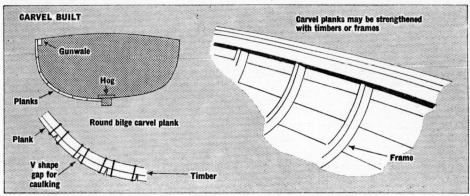

In round bilge boats the planks are shaped to form the curve of the hull and a little V-shaped gap is left between each plank. This has to be filled or CAULKED with caulking cotton, bedding paint and cement filler. The carvel planking is strengthened on the inside of the hull with timbers in the same way as clinker planking. A more recent development is to fit the planks very closely and leave them square faced without caulking. The planks swell after launching and close up tight.

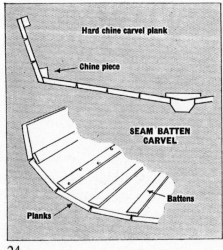

In hard chine boats the planks lie flat. They are stiffened on the inside by frames which are stronger than timbers and spaced further apart. Where two planks join, a batten running fore and aft is let into the frames and nailed or glued to both planks.

This construction is known as SEAM BATTEN or RIBBAND CARVEL.

The same kind of wood is used as for clinker planking.

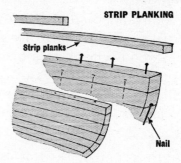

STRIP PLANKING

STRIP PLANKING is a special form of carvel planking. The planks are reduced in width until they are almost *square*. They run fore and aft and are placed edge to edge as in traditional carvel-built. They are nailed from the top surface of the strip into the plank or strip below.

DOUBLE SKIN hulls have two thicknesses of planking glued together. The combined double skin is the same thickness as a single skin or perhaps a little thicker.

Both skins are sometimes arranged so that the planks run fore and aft as in clinker and carvel planking. Another method is for the outer planks to run fore and aft while the planks of the inner skin run diagonally across those of the outer skin. This is known as SINGLE DIAGONAL PLANKING. When the planks of both skins are set diagonally the planking is known as DOUBLE DIAGONAL.

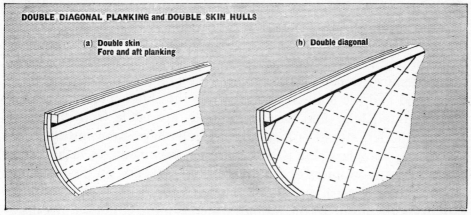

DOUBLE DIAGONAL PLANKING and DOUBLE SKIN HULLS

(a) Double skin Fore and aft planking

(b) Double diagonal

SHEET PLYWOOD is used more for hard chine than round bilge boats. By a recent discovery it is possible to curve plywood panels in two directions and in future SHEET PLYWOOD may be used more frequently for round bilge boats. The panels must be of good quality plywood made specially for marine use such as RESIN BONDED PLYWOOD made to British Standard Specifications BS1088 and AX100.

The panels are glued together with resin or synthetic glue. Lengthways the plywood is sometimes joined with BUTT STRAPS or SCARFED.

Many internationally famous racing dinghy classes are built of MOULDED PLYWOOD by gluing down layer after layer of strips of thin wood veneers on a boat-shaped mould. The veneers may be hot moulded in autoclaves or cold moulded, i.e. pinned and glued. The hull that results needs no framing at all and is light, smooth and easy to care for. This is a mass-production technique.

Metal

SHEET STEEL or IRON is used for most large commercial vessels and iron yachts. Overlapping sheets of steel or iron plates are built up on a girder frame and are riveted or welded to it.

LIGHT ALLOYS are used for small boats and some larger craft. In boats of hard chine construction the metal sheets are used in the same way as plywood. They are riveted together and strengthened by a metal frame. Light alloys are also moulded to form.

Fibreglass

Used mainly for dinghies and yacht tenders. Some larger yachts, particularly one-design racing boats, have been built of fibre-glass and its use is spreading to commercial craft. This new material is made of glass fibres in the form of scrim, mat or cloth held together with resin glue so that it forms a skin. Polyester or epoxy are the most common types of resin. A catalyst is used to change polyester and epoxy resins chemically. The maker's specification on the amount of catalyst to be used and the temperature at which the skin is cured is critical.

Both round bilge and hard chine hulls are made from fibreglass. First a wooden mould is made of the hull shape by using strip plywood. The fibreglass skin is laid on either the outside or inside of the mould. The smoothness of the finished hull depends on the quality of the mould and one side of the skin is left with a rough finish and if it is built on the inside of the mould, which is more common, the inside of the skin is left rough.

Fibreglass is fairly expensive because of the cost of the resins and cloth and the extra labour for building the mould, but it has many advantages. It is light, strong, and very hard-wearing. It needs a major accident to do damage. There is very little maintenance to be done except scrubbing. Painting is unnecessary because the colouring agent is in the resin, and the material does not require the protection normally given by paint. Another advantage is that fibreglass does not absorb water so that the weight of the hull remains constant when afloat. In addition fibreglass is very useful for repairing old boats.

Hull performance and shape

The performance of the hull depends on its shape and measurements.

Shape

The shape of the bows, stern, underwater sections and sheerline influences the behaviour of the boat.

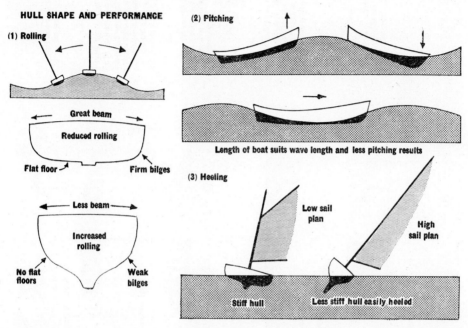

The SHEERLINE is the outline at the top edge of the hull when you look at it from the side. It is usually a gentle, curved line with its lowest part just astern of midships and its highest part forward.

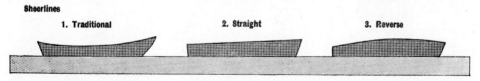

STRAIGHT SHEERLINES and REVERSE SHEER have recently been introduced. Reverse sheer gives more headroom amidships for cruising yachts.

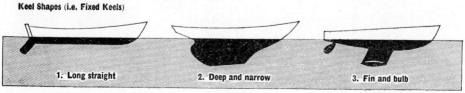

27

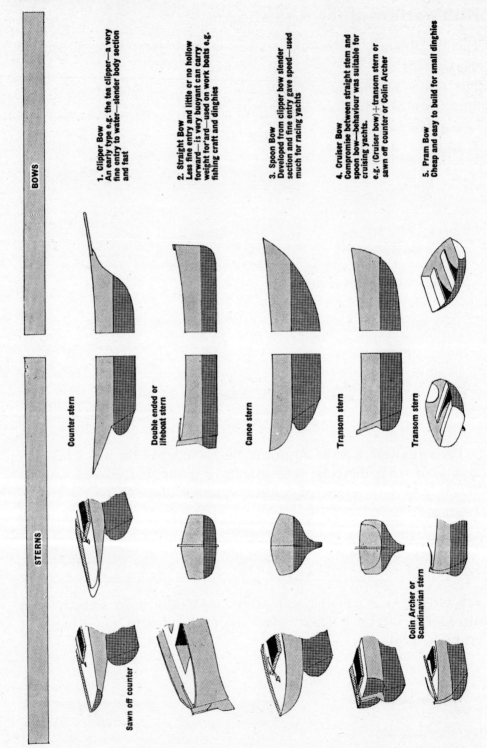

BOWS

1. Clipper Bow
An early type e.g. the tea clipper—a very fine entry to water—slender body section and fast

2. Straight Bow
Less fine entry and little or no hollow forward—is very buoyant can carry weight for'ard—used on work boats e.g. fishing craft and dinghies

3. Spoon Bow
Developed from clipper bow slender section and fine entry gave speed—used much for racing yachts

4. Cruiser Bow
Compromise between straight stem and spoon bow—behaviour was suitable for cruising yachts.
e.g. (Cruiser bow)+transom stern or sawn off counter or Colin Archer

5. Pram Bow
Cheap and easy to build for small dinghies

STERNS

Counter stern

Double ended or lifeboat stern

Canoe stern

Transom stern

Transom stern

Sawn off counter

Colin Archer or Scandinavian stern

Measurement

There are four principal measurements:

   (i)   Length   (ii)   Beam   (iii)   Draught   (iv)   Size or tonnage

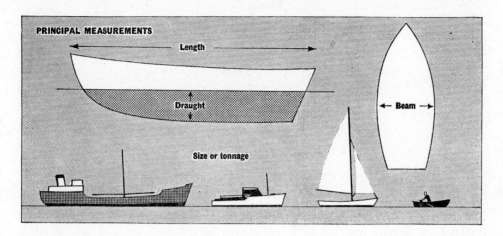

PRINCIPAL MEASUREMENTS

Length

Draught

Beam

Size or tonnage

(i) Length

The LENGTH is described in three ways.

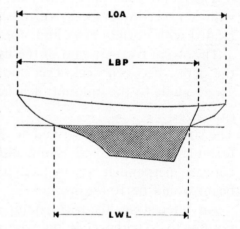

LOA = Length overall, from the for'ard tip of the bowsprit or bows, if there is no bowsprit, to the furthest point aft.

LBP = Length between perpendiculars, from the foreside of the stem to the aft side of the sternpost or transom.

LWL = Length on the water-line.

(ii) Beam

The BEAM is the maximum width of the hull.

(iii) Draught

The DRAUGHT of a vessel is her depth below the water-line and it varies with the size, shape, and position of her keel and her loading and trim. It is measured in feet and the vessel is said to draw, for example, 5 feet.

29

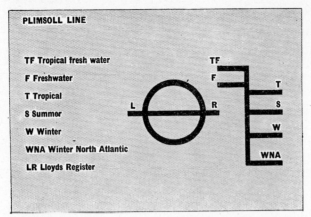

PLIMSOLL LINE

TF Tropical fresh water
F Freshwater
T Tropical
S Summer
W Winter
WNA Winter North Atlantic
LR Lloyds Register

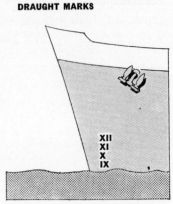

DRAUGHT MARKS

Commercial vessels carry DRAUGHT MARKS painted at the bows and stern to show what they are drawing at a particular time. They also carry the PLIMSOLL line painted on their topsides to show the maximum depth for loading cargoes, depending on sea areas and seasons. Samuel Plimsoll, M.P., introduced the control of loading of commercial vessels to Parliament in the Merchant Shipping Act of 1876.

Yachts do not usually carry draught-marks but the hull is painted with a LOAD WATER-LINE to show where the vessel floats when loaded with normal crew and stores.

The MOULDED DEPTH of the hull is important to yachtsmen. It is the depth between deck-level and keelson and in cabin yachts will give a guide to the amount of headroom available.

(iv) Size

The size of yachts is described according to THAMES TONNAGE. The formula is $\frac{(L-B) \times B \times \frac{1}{2}B}{94}$. B is maximum beam in feet and L is length between perpendiculars in feet, for example, a 30-footer of 10 feet beam would be 10·6 tons.

An interesting historical point is that tonnage in this sense has nothing to do with weight but was originally an estimate of the number of tuns of wine a ship would carry.

Relationship between measurements

The relationship between measurements is also important and affects the efficiency of the hull. The relationship between maximum beam and length, the draught and length, and the length and speed will vary according to the type of boat. This is a general guide for pleasure-craft under sail to which there are exceptions.

RELATIONSHIP BETWEEN MEASUREMENTS

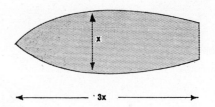

BEAM-LENGTH RATIO
Length is about three times beam.

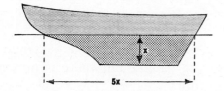

DRAUGHT-LENGTH RATIO
Excluding centre-board craft, draught is about $\frac{1}{5}$ of water-line length.

LENGTH-SPEED RATIO
For hulls which do not plane or skim over the water, the maximum speed of a hull is about $1\cdot2\times$ the root of the water-line length expressed in knots. A boat 25 feet on the water-line, $1\cdot2\times\sqrt{25}=1\cdot2\times5=6\cdot0$ knots maximum speed.

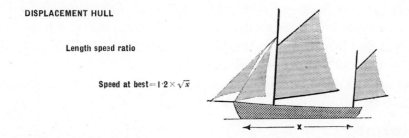

DISPLACEMENT HULL

Length speed ratio

Speed at best $= 1\cdot2\times\sqrt{x}$

A boat that planes travels much faster, sailing about 1 knot per foot of water-line length at best.

PLANING HULL

May be a knot to every foot of water-line length

5. Sails—the Heart of a Boat

'The age of sail is past.' This is true of the trading and passenger vessels, and the large cruising and racing yachts, but there is now a new age of sail, the era of small-boat sailors.

Sails are the heart of a sailing boat. They are as important to a boat as a mainspring to a watch. Study them carefully. Know how to use them and how to look after them. Sails are not only expensive but the efficiency of your boat will depend on them.

The sailmaker has a language of his own. If you know this language you will be better able to handle your sails.

Materials

The materials from which sails are made are:

(1) Sailcloth made from:
    (*a*) synthetic fibres;
    (*b*) natural fibres.
(2) Rope.
(3) Wire and metal fittings.
(4) Sewing thread and twine.

Synthetic fibres—'TERYLENE' or 'DACRON' polyester fibre and NYLON

These fibres are produced by chemical methods. 'TERYLENE' sails are becoming popular for all types of sailing boat. The advantages of 'Terylene' sails over cotton are given in the table. 'DACRON' is the American equivalent of Terylene. NYLON has been superseded by 'Terylene' except for spinnakers. For racing, synthetic sails, 'Terylene' for standing sails and nylon for spinnakers, are now used for all new craft and replacement sails. The use of cotton is becoming the exception.

32

Natural fibres—flax and cotton

In Europe FLAX was used at first and most commercial sailing vessels had flax sails. Many cruising yachts still have flax sails, but small craft and racing boats use COTTON. The merits and characteristics of flax and cotton sails are given in the Table.

FLAX	COTTON	'TERYLENE'
Does not tear easily	Tears more easily	Very tough—does not tear
Slightly greasy and does not mildew easily	More liable to attack by mildew	Almost impervious to water
		Fibres do not absorb water—do not rot or mildew
Rough texture that disturbs airflow	Better texture—better airflow	Very fine smooth texture that improves airflow
Shrinks excessively when wet	Also shrinks and becomes distorted when wet	Extremely hard wearing—does not stretch easily—does not shrink
Does not keep shape well	Keeps shape better and longer	Keeps shape well—has long life
Heavy and stiff, awkward to handle	Lighter and more easily handled	Light and easy to handle but slippery
Cheap	More expensive	Initially expensive

In the main, American and Egyptian cotton is used for sail-making.

Flax and cotton sailcoths are measured in three ways, by width, length, and weight.

Widths. Sailcoths are made in widths varying from 15 to 36 inches. When making up the sails the wider cloths have to be split down the middle or false seams put in. It is quite common now for the cloth as seen in the made-up sail to be called a panel.

Length. The cotton cloths come from a BOLT of cotton material measuring anything from 40 to 100 yards in length.

Weight. The weight of the sailcoth runs from 2 oz. to 28 oz. per square yard. The lighter cloths are used for small boats. Heavier cloths are used for larger craft, particularly cruising vessels. The sails of work boats used to be made of heavy cloths.

Rope

A great deal of rope is used in the making of a sail. This rope is known as the BOLT ROPE. The diagram shows where it is sewn on to the sail

33

and the names of its various parts. When sails are hoisted and set the tension and strain is taken mainly by the bolt rope. The size of a rope is given as its circumference in inches. The breaking strain of best Italian hemp is the $\frac{\text{circumference}^2}{3}$ tons. The safe working load is half this for an occasional load. For regular use $\frac{1}{6}$ of breaking strain is a safe limit.

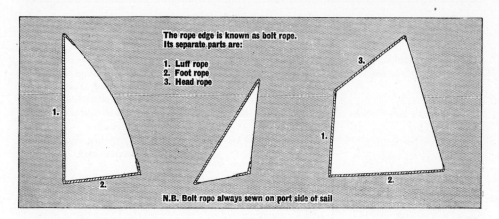

The rope edge is known as bolt rope. Its separate parts are:

1. Luff rope
2. Foot rope
3. Head rope

N.B. Bolt rope always sewn on port side of sail

Manila rope was almost the only rope used in the past. Today it is not used so much. It is made from the fibres of banana leaves mainly from the Philippines.

Italian hemp is a little stronger, wears well and lasts much longer. It is very smooth and unlike cotton rope does not get hard when wet. Italian hemp is often lightly tarred for sail-making. It is almost the only rope now used in the making of cotton sails.

'Terylene' and Nylon bolt ropes are used if the sailcloth is made from the new synthetic fibres. The cloth and the rope edging the cloth then have practically the same stretch. 'Terylene' and Nylon ropes are produced for this and other purposes. In the same way, 'Terylene' and Nylon sails must be made up with synthetic sewing threads as cotton sewing will shrink when affected by water and thus distort the seams.

Wire and metal fittings

A flexible galvanized or stainless steel wire is often used instead of rope for the leading edge of headsails. It is sometimes used in the leading edge of Bermudan mainsails, but it is more common in this case for the wire to be in addition to the rope. When setting the sail this wire prevents the bolt rope from being overstretched.

34

Metal fittings include THIMBLES of various shapes, EYELETS and PISTON HANKS. They are made of brass or galvanized iron.

A Bermudan mainsail also has a HEADBOARD, as shown on page 37. Most headboards are now made of light alloy. In the past they were made of wood.

WIRE AND METAL FITTINGS

1. MAST TRACK AND SLIDES

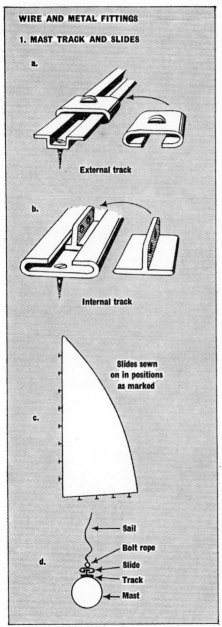

a.

External track

b.

Internal track

c.

Slides sewn on in positions as marked

d.

Sail
Bolt rope
Slide
Track
Mast

2. THIMBLES

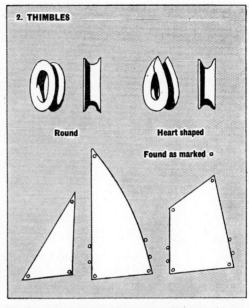

Round

Heart shaped

Found as marked o

3. PISTON HANKS

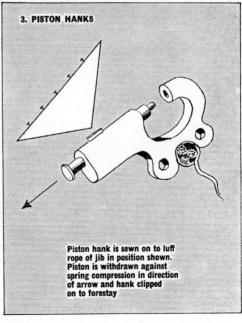

Piston hank is sewn on to luff rope of jib in position shown. Piston is withdrawn against spring compression in direction of arrow and hank clipped on to forestay

Parts of a Sail

Through the years sailmakers and seamen have given interesting names to the various parts of sails. Some names refer to locations or particular areas of the sail while others refer to the construction of the sail.

It is as useful to know the parts of mainsails and headsails as it is to know the parts of a boat's hull.

1. LINES AND AREAS

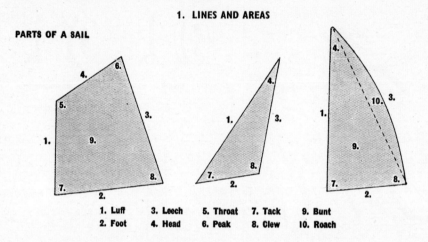

PARTS OF A SAIL

1. Luff	3. Leech	5. Throat	7. Tack	9. Bunt
2. Foot	4. Head	6. Peak	8. Clew	10. Roach

2. PARTS TO DO WITH CONSTRUCTION (No bolt rope shown, see illustration on page 34)

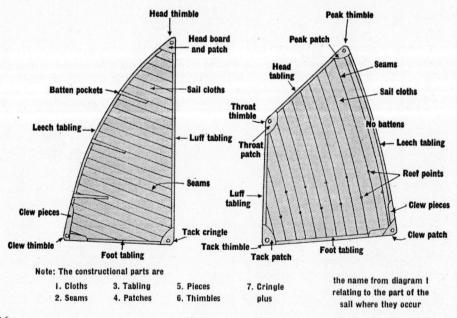

Note: The constructional parts are

1. Cloths	3. Tabling	5. Pieces	7. Cringle	the name from diagram 1
2. Seams	4. Patches	6. Thimbles	plus	relating to the part of the sail where they occur

PARTS OF A SAIL

HEADBOARD   CLEW   TACK

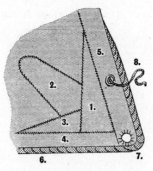
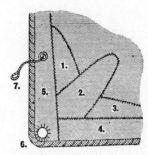

1. Headboard sewn inside sailcloth
2. Gunmetal plate for shackling halyard
3. Stitching
4. Leech tabling
5. Luff rope—top whipped and gap to headboard to allow sail to pass up luff groove in mast
6. Leech line comes out of tabling through eyelet

1, 2, 3. Reinforcing patches
4. Foot tabling
5. Leech tabling
6. Foot rope continued around clew and a little way up leech
7. Clew cringle
8. Leech line

1, 2, 3. Reinforcing patches
4. Foot tabling
5. Luff tabling
6. Tack cringle
7. Luff tension wire

RECAP

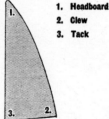

1. Headboard
2. Clew
3. Tack

The cut of sails

Sails have been made for many centuries all over the world by sewing up strips of sailcloth. The sailcloths are set out and stitched up in four well-developed patterns. The way in which the cloths are put together is described as the CUT OF SAILS.

The four standard methods are named from the way in which the panels of cloth run in sails. They are:

(1) The vertical cut.   (3) The diagonal cut.

(2) The horizontal or cross cut.   (4) The Scottish cut.

37

1. Vertical cut

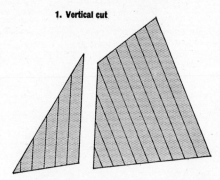

In the VERTICAL CUT the cloths run parallel to the leech. This is the oldest method of construction. It works particularly well for a lugsail or gaff mainsail and mizzen because it reduces bagginess in the area of the leech and roach.

In the HORIZONTAL or CROSS CUT the panels of cloth run at right angles to the leech. This cut is used in the mainsails of most modern yachts, particularly Bermudan-rigged boats and racing craft. The seams and airflow run in the same direction and there appears to be a better airflow.

2. Horizontal or cross cut

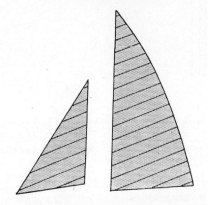

3. Diagonal or mitre cut

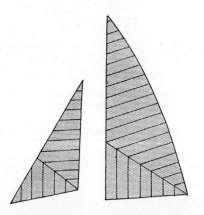

In the DIAGONAL or MITRE CUT the sail is divided into two parts by the LAST, which is the line that bisects the angle at the clew of the sail. Above the last the cloths run at right angles to the leech and below the last at right angles to the foot. Sails with a diagonal cut keep their shape well. They are usually fitted with a wire luff rope. The diagonal cut is mainly used for headsails, but it is occasionally used for Bermudan mainsails.

In the SCOTTISH CUT as well, the last again is used to divide the sail into two parts. The cloths run parallel to the leech and foot. In the past the headsails of most commercial vessels were cut in this way.

4. Scottish cut

38

Various other ways of cutting and sewing cloths

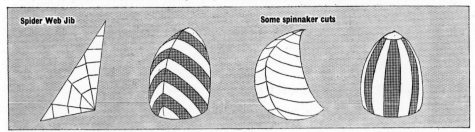

Spider Web Jib

Some spinnaker cuts

Shape in a sail

When set in a breeze a sail has a gently varying curve over its whole area. Like the peel of an orange, a sail will never lie flat. Looked at from above the curve in a sail is that of an AEROFOIL.

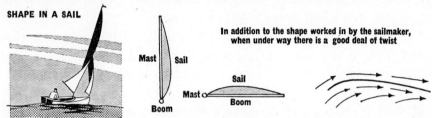

SHAPE IN A SAIL

Mast   Sail

Boom

In addition to the shape worked in by the sailmaker, when under way there is a good deal of twist

Sail

Mast   Boom

This shape is worked in by the sailmaker when he cuts the sail and afterwards sews it up. Four ROACHES or curves are put in along the edges of a gaff mainsail and three in a Bermudan or other triangular sail. Except along the after edge of the sail, these curves which are supported by the bolt rope are pulled straight when a mainsail is bent to its mast and spars and the bolt rope put under tension. They pass on their curvature to the rest of the sail and the result is the aerofoil shape. The hollow in the sail is known as the BUNT or BELLY.

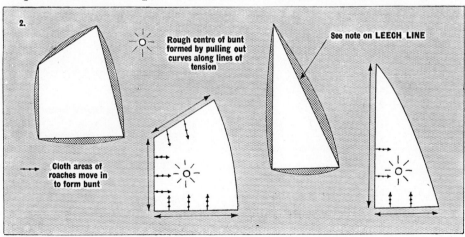

2.

Rough centre of bunt formed by pulling out curves along lines of tension

See note on LEECH LINE

Cloth areas of roaches move in to form bunt

A badly stretched sail either develops FLATS or localized bagginess which destroys its perfect shape and reduces its efficiency. This happens when you do not ease the fastenings of a sail that is shrinking rapidly through becoming wet at sea.

Reef points and reefing

To REEF a sail is to reduce its area to offset heavy seas and strong winds. This chapter deals with reefing in relation to the construction of sails. When and how to reef is explained later.

The older method of reefing is to bundle the sail down neatly on top of the boom or to the bolt rope if there is no boom. It is then secured in this position by tying the reef points round the foot rope, using a reef knot, but *never* round the boom.

REEF POINTS are made up of a line of little square PATCHES sewn on each side of the sail nearly parallel to the foot. On some sails the patches are fitted with eyelets through which LACING LINE or SEPARATE TIES can be passed and secured. On other sails, PENNANTS about 6 to 9 inches long are sewn through the patches and remain permanently fixed on the sail. There are usually two and sometimes three lines of reef points which are staggered. CRINGLES at the luff rope and leech of the sail correspond to the lines of reef points and take the strain when tying down a reef.

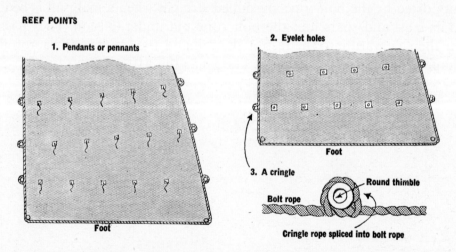

REEF POINTS

1. Pendants or pennants

Foot

2. Eyelet holes

Foot

3. A cringle

Bolt rope

Round thimble

Cringle rope spliced into bolt rope

ROLLER REEFING is another method of reefing a mainsail by rolling the boom with the sail round it. When this method is used there are no reef points on the sail.

40

Attaching mainsail to mast and spars

LACING THE SAIL is the oldest method but it is now used less and less. The TABLING at the edge of the sail is fitted with eyelet holes through which lacing line or separate tiers are passed to secure the sail to the spar. Separate tiers are better because if the lacing line chafes in one place the whole lot may carry away. Note the difference between lacing to a mast, in which case the sail moves up the mast when hoisting, and to a gaff or boom, where the sail does not move.

ATTACHING MAINSAIL TO MAST AND SPARS

1. Gaff or gunter mainsail to mast

Mast

Mainsail

Luff rope

Eyelet holes

Luff tabling

Lacing line

Masts hoops

Gaff

Gaff mainsail

Masts

Boom

2. Mainsail to spar (boom)

Sail

Boom

Simplest but not a very good method.

Earing

3. Mainsail to spar (gaff)

Gaff

A better method for both gaff and boom

Sail

4. Mainsail to spar (boom)

Sail

Boom

Use of individual tie ropes at each eyelet hole. Very seamanlike and safe.

Rarely seen today. Hoops around the mast to attach main sail to it.

41

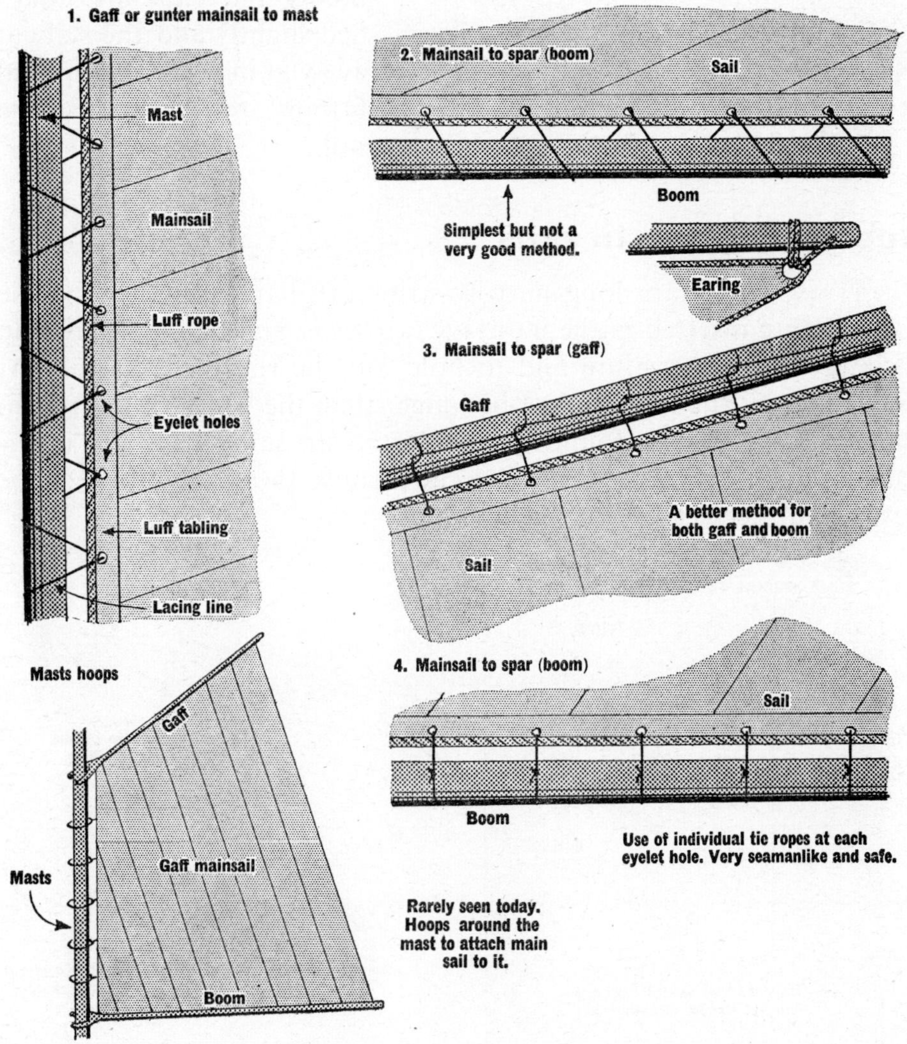

In the second method a METAL TRACK is attached to the mast or spar and TRACK SLIDES are attached to the sail, as shown on page 35. The slides are either sewn into the bolt rope or they have eyelets or GROMMETS. Gun-metal was used a great deal in the past for tracks and slides but the use of light alloy and plastic is now more common.

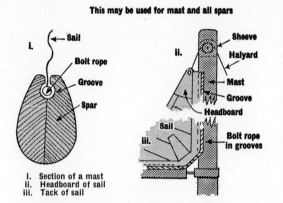

This may be used for mast and all spars

i. Section of a mast
ii. Headboard of sail
iii. Tack of sail

In the third method masts and spars are GROOVED so that the bolt rope at the edge of the sail is passed inside the GROOVE. When this method is used the headboard and clew are modified slightly and the sail cut away at the tack. No special fittings are required on the sail.

Special feature in sails

BATTENS, which are long narrow strips of pliable wood or plastic material, are inserted in the BATTEN POCKETS and tied in. They help to improve the curvature and to hold out the roach of the sail. At any one point the batten must be longer than the width of the roach. Battens are normally found on all Bermudan sails. They are rarely found on gaff sails with a vertical cut because these keep their shape better and the area of the roach is less.

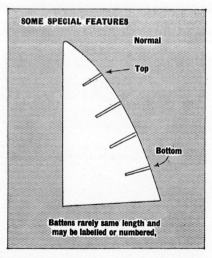

SOME SPECIAL FEATURES

Battens rarely same length and may be labelled or numbered.

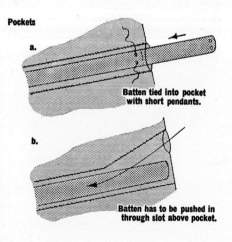

Pockets

a. Batten tied into pocket with short pendants.

b. Batten has to be pushed in through slot above pocket.

The latest development is to produce fully battened sails, like the sails which have been common in east and south-east Asia for centuries. The aerofoil shape of the sail is improved, the sail keeps its shape better for a longer period and the airflow is much more efficient.

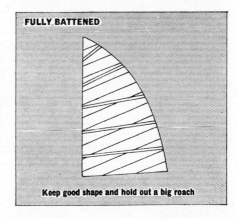

FULLY BATTENED

Keep good shape and hold out a big roach

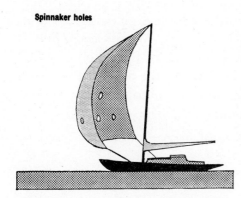

Spinnaker holes

SPINNAKER HOLES are circular vents in spinnaker sails used when the wind is blowing from behind the boat to improve efficiency. After its impact on the sail, the force of the wind is spent. The used air has to be got rid of and these holes speed up the flow of escaping air from the bunt of the spinnaker.

Large overlapping Genoa foresails and mainsails on low booms make it difficult for the helmsman to see ahead and to leeward. To get over this difficulty mainsails and foresails have appeared with fairly large WINDOWS cut in them. These windows are usually made of 'MELINEX' polyester film. They prove very efficient but it is not a common practice as yet.

Windows

43

Leech line

A line known as a LEECH LINE runs from the *Headboard* to the *Clew* and is free to move inside the tabling of the sail. The object is to control the amount of belly in the sail according to the weather. In light airs the leech line must be tightened to increase the bunt while in strong winds the leech line should be let out to flatten the bunt.

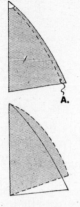

(1) **Position.** Leech line is in position as shown inside tabling at the leech. It is fixed at the headboard and comes out through the eyelet hole near the clew at A.

(2) **Effect.** (*a*) When the leech line is let out loosely the sail sets rather flatter, i.e. with less bunt as in shaded sail. (*b*) When leech line is tightened up the curve of the roach is pulled into a straight line and the area of the roach has to pass on into the middle of the sail and give more bunt.

(3) **Control.** By means of a stopper knot at A—either overhand or figure of eight.

6. Rigging

Spars

The diagram shows the position of masts and spars in a boat and the progress made in making spars lighter and stronger. Wooden spars used to be solid. Originally they were made of grown timbers or their limbs. Laminated spars made of planks of wood glued together were developed later. As they were stronger they could be made lighter.

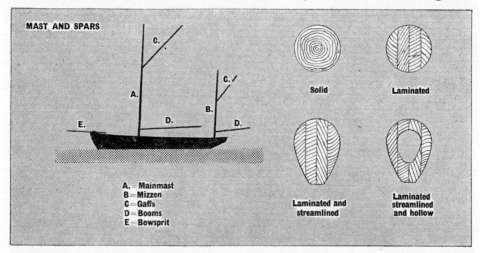

MAST AND SPARS

Solid

Laminated

Laminated and streamlined

Laminated streamlined and hollow

A. = Mainmast
B = Mizzen
C = Gaffs
D = Booms
E = Bowsprit

It was discovered that hollow spars would be even stronger and lighter. In recent years it has been possible to make hollow spars of special alluminium alloys that are light and are not corroded by seawater. Both masts and sails have to stand winds up to gale force and the hulls, on which they are stepped, are often driven hard by their skippers in rough seas.

Standing rigging

Masts have to be supported efficiently. The arrangement of wire and rope by which this is done is called STANDING RIGGING. In larger craft standing rigging once set up is rarely adjusted. Small dinghy owners may have to strip down and set up the rigging each trip.

Standing rigging is usually made of flexible wire for which different types of steel are used:

STAINLESS STEEL which has a high nickel content.

PLOUGH STEEL which has a higher carbon content than mild steel, is stronger and more easily tempered.

ROD STEEL which is like piano wire.

Except when the mast is lowered for refitting or for any other purpose, the rigging stands until it is renewed because of wear or old age.

Masts supported by forestays, backstays and shrouds

Some masts are supported in the fore and aft direction by FORE-STAYS in front of the mast and by BACKSTAYS aft of the mast. Athwartships, that is, across the beam of the boat, masts are supported by stays known as SHROUDS.

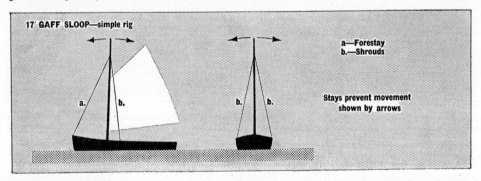

17' GAFF SLOOP—simple rig

a—Forestay
b.—Shrouds

Stays prevent movement shown by arrows

Unstayed masts

Some boats do not require stays. The masts are described as UN-STAYED. In the past even quite big boats, like the Norwegian pilot cutters, had very stout masts nearly a foot in diameter, and did without standing rigging. Lugsail dinghies up to about 12 feet in length do not have stays. Modern racing dinghies, like the Olympic single-handed boat, the Finn and the *Yachting World* Solo have no standing rigging. This is possible because of the strength of their hollow, laminated spars. They have the advantage that without standing rigging there is less interference with the flow of air along the sails.

46

Second pair of shrouds

A second pair of shrouds carried further aft will both support the mast and also prevent it from moving forward. The tendency for the mast to move forward is created in two ways; with the wind aft, by pressure of the wind and with the wind for'ard, by the pull of the jib when it is full of wind.

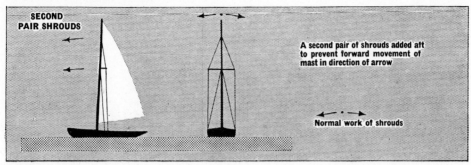

SECOND PAIR SHROUDS

A second pair of shrouds added aft to prevent forward movement of mast in direction of arrow

Normal work of shrouds

Running backstays

When you sail with the wind aft, the boom and sail should be as far forward as possible and the boom should be nearly at right angles to the mast in the fore-and-aft line. If backstays were fixed permanently from the mast to the side of the hull, the sail and boom would catch against them and prevent this. To overcome the difficulty backstays are made to move at deck level and they are known as SLIDING or RUNNING BACKSTAYS. The backstay slides fore and aft on a wire stay or length of track. The running backstay on the side opposite the boom and sail should always be taut or, in other words, set up. The backstay on the same side of the boat as the boom and sail should be slackened off so that it does not restrict the movement of the sail.

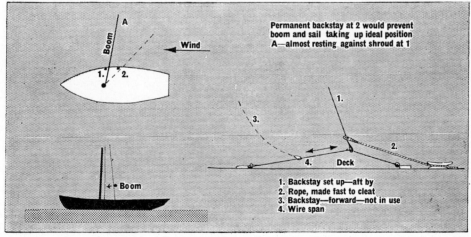

A

Boom

Wind

Permanent backstay at 2 would prevent boom and sail taking up ideal position A—almost resting against shroud at 1

1. 2.

1.

3.

2.

4. Deck

Boom

1. Backstay set up—aft by
2. Rope, made fast to cleat
3. Backstay—forward—not in use
4. Wire span

Fixed backstay

In place of two running backstays, boats with an inboard rig are often fitted with a single FIXED BACKSTAY. This makes it easier to handle the boat under way. If it is necessary to carry this backstay a little further aft to clear the mainsail this is done with a bumkin. A single standing backstay is often split right aft to avoid interfering with the rudder head and tiller.

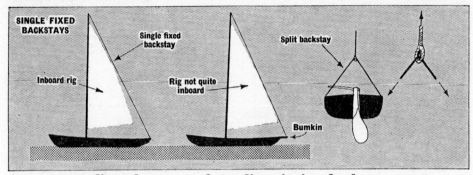

A more complicated pattern of standing rigging for longer masts

A Bermudan-rigged boat with an increased sail area and longer mast needs more standing rigging.

On a 16-foot Bermudan sloop with a 100 square feet of mainsail, the mast is about 25 feet in length. This long mast has increased strain. To balance this a second forestay, the FORETOPMAST STAY, and a pair of UPPER SHROUDS fitted with CROSSTREES is necessary. Crosstrees are struts made of a wood or light alloy and set athwart the mast to spread the upper shrouds. As an alternative, JUMPER STRUTS and stays are sometimes added instead of the upper forestay, and DIAMOND STAYS and struts in place of the upper shrouds.

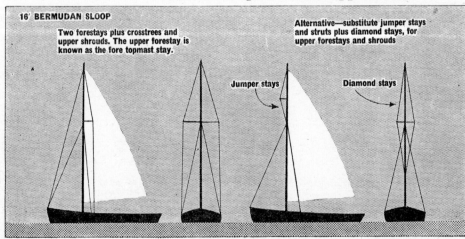

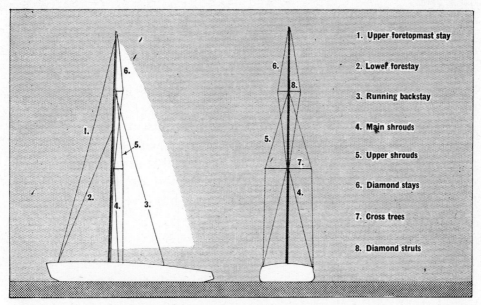

1. Upper foretopmast stay

2. Lower forestay

3. Running backstay

4. Main shrouds

5. Upper shrouds

6. Diamond stays

7. Cross trees

8. Diamond struts

In an 18-foot Bermudan sloop with 200 square feet of sail and a hollow laminated mast not more than $3\frac{1}{2}$ inches in diameter the standing rigging is still more complicated.

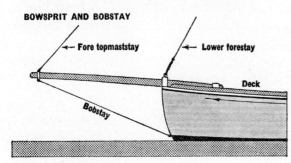

BOWSPRIT AND BOBSTAY

←— Fore topmaststay   ←— Lower forestay

Deck

Bobstay

A **Bobstay** helps to hold down the bowsprit or bumkin.

Running rigging

As the name implies, RUNNING RIGGING is constantly being adjusted. It does not remain fixed like standing rigging. Running rigging is the term given to the ropes by which the sails are hoisted, set and trimmed. To trim is to adjust the sails when the wind changes or the boat alters course. To hoist and to trim are two different operations. They require two main types of running rigging for each function:

Halyards for hoisting sail. This comes from haulyard. Earlier spelling halliard.

Sheets for trimming sail.

49

Halyards

HALYARDS hoist aloft the head of the sail and therefore need to be connected with the top of the mast. This is done in one of two ways: (1) they are ROVE through a BLOCK attached to the mast by a STROP or shackled to a mast band. Rove is the past tense of the verb to reeve—to pass a rope through a hole or block; (2) they are passed over a SHEAVE and down through a hollow mast to deck level.

Halyards are made of rope or flexible steel wire or partly of rope and partly of wire. The rope may be of vegetable fibre such as cotton or hemp or of synthetic fibre such as Nylon or Terylene. If the flexible wire is stainless it is expensive but it has a very long life.

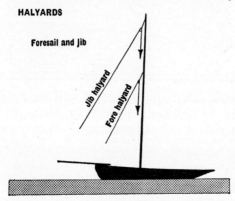

HALYARDS

Foresail and Jib

Jib halyard

Fore halyard

Fore Halyards or **Jib Halyards** are halyards for'ard of the mast for hoisting headsails. If a boat has a spinnaker then a **spinnaker halyard** is used.

A Bermudan mainsail is hoisted with a MAIN HALYARD. This halyard passes over a sheave let into the top of the mast and then either inside or outside the mast down to deck level. Halyards that are led inside a hollow mast are known as INTERNAL HALYARDS.

A gunter mainsail may have one main halyard attached to the gaff. The position where it is attached must be exactly right if the sail is to set well. This point is often tricky to find. Another difficulty is that when reefing, the sail will not set properly without altering the position of this point.

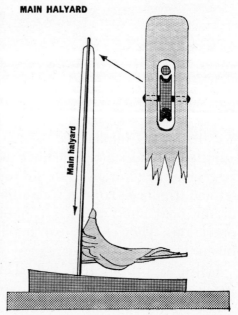

MAIN HALYARD

Main halyard

50

It is better if the gunter mainsail is hoisted with two halyards in the same way as a gaff mainsail. These are the THROAT and PEAK HAL-YARDS. The wire span on the gaff to which the peak halyard is attached is called a JACKSTAY. This allows the halyard to adjust its position automatically in relation to the gaff when setting sail and when reefing.

A lugsail only requires one halyard but the sail is often held close against the mast by a rope downhaul, which is called a BRAIL.

Flag halyards, signal halyards or lines are required to hoist the burgee and all flags.

PEAK AND THROAT HALYARDS

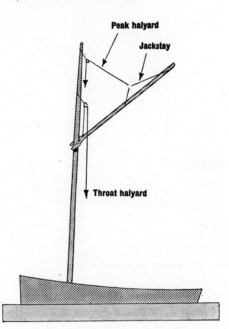

Peak halyard
Jackstay
Throat halyard

LUGSAIL

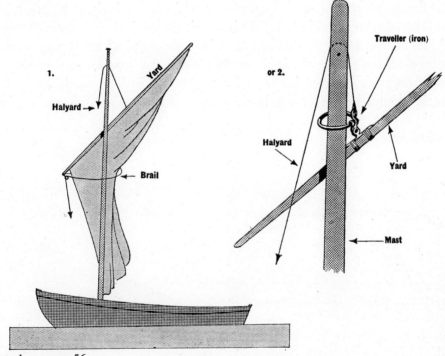

1.
Halyard →
Yard
← Brail

or 2.
Traveller (iron)
Halyard
Yard
←—— Mast

See also page 56.

51

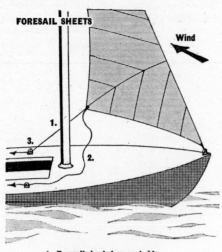

FORESAIL SHEETS

Wind

1. Foresail sheeted on port side
2. Sheet idle and hanging loose on starboard (windward) side •
3. Sheets run aft through fairleads on deck

Sheets

Sheets are the ropes used to trim the sails when under way. They take their names from the sails which they control, thus the jib is controlled by the JIB SHEET.

Every headsail sheet is in two parts—one for working each side of the boat. The two parts of the sheet are usually run through FAIRLEADS on deck and so brought inboard. A sail is sheeted on the lee side of the boat, i.e. the opposite side from that on which the wind is blowing. With a head-sail, the sheet on the non-working side, i.e. to windward, will lie idle and hang loose.

The mainsail is controlled by the MAINSHEET. Often a very large sail has to be managed single-handed with the mainsheet in one hand and the tiller in the other. To achieve this the mainsheet is rove through blocks to obtain a purchase and gain a mechanical advantage which at least halves the work. Such an arrangement is known as a TACKLE, pronounced takel. Notice from where the mainsheet leads and what mechanical advantage is gained.

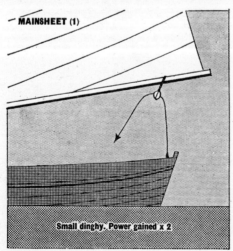

MAINSHEET (1)

Small dinghy. Power gained x 2

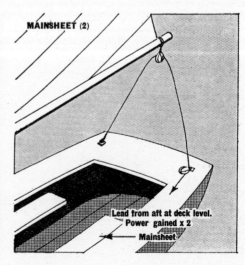

MAINSHEET (2)

Lead from aft at deck level.
Power gained x 2
Mainsheet

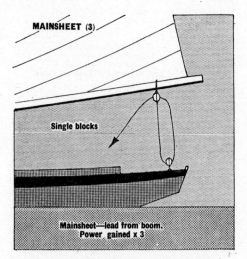

MAINSHEET (3)

Single blocks

Mainsheet—lead from boom.
Power gained x 3

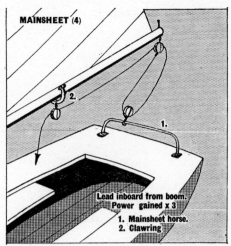

MAINSHEET (4)

Lead inboard from boom.
Power gained x 3
1. Mainsheet horse.
2. Clawring

Other running rigging

Sailing boats often have other items of running rigging.

Many boats are fitted with LIFTING RUDDERS. The chief advantage is that they can be raised when sailing in shallow water. To adjust the position these rudders are fitted with a hoist made of rope or of flexible wire with a rope tail. If the rudder blade is made of wood and is unballasted then the rope is arranged to heave down the rudder and keep it down as required.

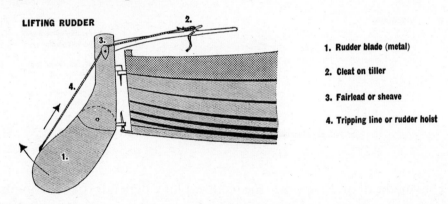

LIFTING RUDDER

1. Rudder blade (metal)
2. Cleat on tiller
3. Fairlead or sheave
4. Tripping line or rudder hoist

Some boats are fitted with drop keels made of iron, centre-plates made of metal, or centre-boards made of wood. They are fitted in a narrow box on the centre-line of the boat forward of midships. They are dropped or raised by a rope or by a flexible wire with a rope end known as a CENTRE-PLATE HOIST.

53

I CENTREBOARD HOISTS

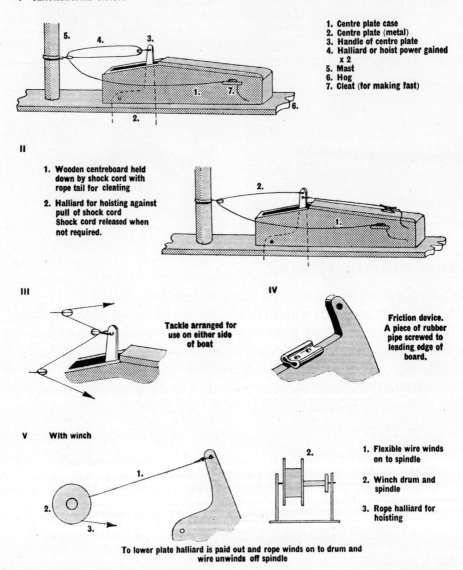

1. Centre plate case
2. Centre plate (metal)
3. Handle of centre plate
4. Halliard or hoist power gained
   x 2
5. Mast
6. Hog
7. Cleat (for making fast)

II

1. Wooden centreboard held
   down by shock cord with
   rope tail for cleating

2. Halliard for hoisting against
   pull of shock cord
   Shock cord released when
   not required.

III

Tackle arranged for
use on either side
of boat

IV

Friction device.
A piece of rubber
pipe screwed to
leading edge of
board.

V   With winch

1. Flexible wire winds
   on to spindle

2. Winch drum and
   spindle

3. Rope halliard for
   hoisting

To lower plate halliard is paid out and rope winds on to drum and
wire unwinds off spindle

The method of dropping the centre-plate depends partly on its
weight and on the material from which it is made. Sometimes a centre-
plate is made of light alloy but often it is made of iron or cast steel
and may weigh anything from 60 to 200 lb. If this is the case, it is
necessary to have a BLOCK-AND-TACKLE to ease the pull on the
hoist when raising the centre-plate. A winch drum is sometimes fitted
as an alternative method.

If the centre-board is made of wood, the hoist is needed to haul down the centre-board and fix it in position because being of wood it is light and will float upwards.

One type of wooden centre-board is fitted with rubber friction pads to hold it down. It is heaved down by hand in the first place, and raised by hand.

When hoisting a sail with a halyard it is difficult to get the luff sufficiently taut to give maximum efficiency. After hoisting the sail and making the halyard fast, this tautness is achieved by using a TACK DOWNHAUL of rope or wire, attached to the tack of the sail, or at the gooseneck, and secured to a cleat on the hull near the mast.

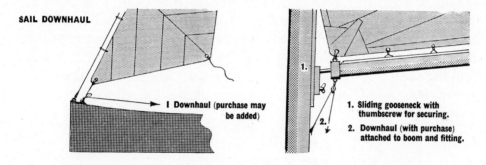

SAIL DOWNHAUL

I Downhaul (purchase may be added)

1. Sliding gooseneck with thumbscrew for securing.
2. Downhaul (with purchase) attached to boom and fitting.

Sometimes this downhaul is fitted with a tackle. As the sails and rope stretch when under way this downhaul has to be adjusted soon after setting out, and again after heavy rain when the ropes shrink.

Boats with heavy booms and big mainsails are often equipped with a **topping lift** which takes the weight of the boom when hoisting and lowering sail and literally TOPS UP THE BOOM. The topping lift is a rope made fast to the after-end of the boom which then leads up to a block or sheave about two-thirds of the way up a Bermudan mast or to the top of a gaff or gunter mast and then down to the foot of the

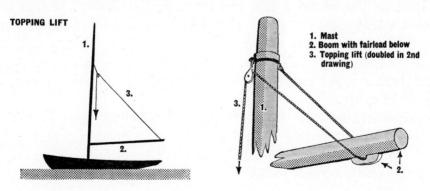

TOPPING LIFT

1.
3.
2.

1. Mast
2. Boom with fairlead below
3. Topping lift (doubled in 2nd drawing)

3.
1.
2.

55

mast. When under way the topping lift is slackened off sufficiently to allow the mainsail to set without interference.

An interesting development on some gaff and gunter rigged boats is that the topping lift is doubled so that it runs on both sides of the boom and sail. The advantage is that when lowering sail in a hurry or single-handed the gaff and sail drop safely between the two parts of the topping lift and rest on the boom. This device also makes it possible to SCANDALIZE the mainsail by topping up the boom in an emergency. To scandalize is to reduce sail by lifting the boom and thereby to spill the wind.

Brails are ropes made fast to the leech of a loose-footed mainsail, usually a lugsail or spritsail. They lead to blocks or BULL'S-EYES on or near the head of the gaff or yard and then to deck level like a halyard. With a spritsail the bull's-eyes are near the throat of the sail although there is no gaff or yard. The ropes are used to TRUSS or haul the sail up to the mast and yard or sprit instead of lowering and stowing the sail. They also provide a quick way of reducing sail in an emergency.

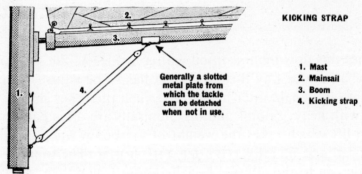

KICKING STRAP

Generally a slotted metal plate from which the tackle can be detached when not in use.

1. Mast
2. Mainsail
3. Boom
4. Kicking strap

Modern racing boats are fitted with KICKING STRAPS. A kicking strap is made of rope or flexible wire with a rope tail and it is fastened to the boom a few feet from the gooseneck. It runs to a point low down on the mast and holds down the boom to prevent it from cocking up when sailing with the wind free. This enables the sail to set flatter with less twist. It is also an aid to safety in broken water because the boom is less likely to gybe or swing from one side to the other.

Small boats may be fitted with a **roller foresail gear** or with a **Wykeham Martin furling gear.** They are not intended for reefing but this works quite well with a roller foresail. The setting and stowing of a foresail or jib is made easier.

56

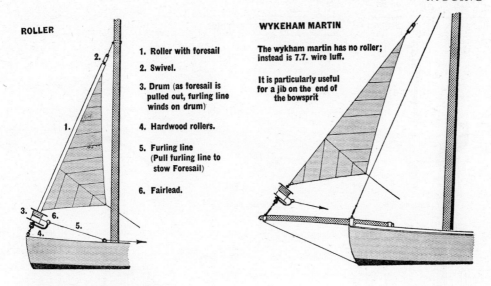

ROLLER

1. Roller with foresail
2. Swivel.
3. Drum (as foresail is pulled out, furling line winds on drum)
4. Hardwood rollers.
5. Furling line (Pull furling line to stow Foresail)
6. Fairlead.

WYKEHAM MARTIN

The wykham martin has no roller; instead is 7.7. wire luff.

It is particularly useful for a jib on the end of the bowsprit

Rigging fittings

(1) Attach: stays to spars and hulls;
　　　　　 halyards to sails and spars;
　　　　　 sheets to sails and booms.
(2) Make fast all items of running rigging.
(3) Enable halyards and sheets to run freely, to change direction and to gain power.

Rigging fittings are made of galvanized iron or stainless steel, gunmetal or wood. Today many synthetic plastic materials are used.

A number of fittings in common use and how they work

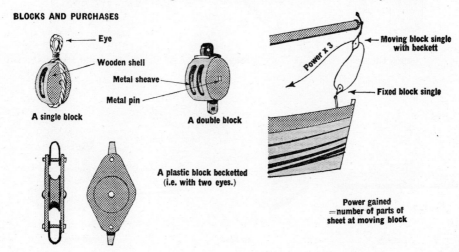

BLOCKS AND PURCHASES

Eye

Wooden shell

Metal sheave

Metal pin

A single block

A double block

A plastic block becketted (i.e. with two eyes.)

Power x 3

Moving block single with beckett

Fixed block single

Power gained =number of parts of sheet at moving block

CLEATS AND FITTINGS

Belaying pin   Ordinary cleat   Jamb cleat

Belaying pins in spider band   Metal cleat   Tufnol jamb cleat

Riding bit   Bottlescrew   Open snatch block

Bullseye   Fairlead   Sheet winch

7. Cordage and Ropework

Different kinds of rope and how they are made

Cordage

ROPE made from FIBRES is known as CORDAGE. It is made from:

(1) Vegetable fibres—Manila, hemp, cotton, sisal, and coir.

(2) Synthetic fibres—Nylon or Terylene.

The fibres are short lengths which are spun into NETTLES. The nettles are twisted together into long lengths to form YARNS. The yarns are then twisted or spun to form STRANDS, which in turn are twisted together to form the rope.

Rope   Strand   Yarns   Fibres

(1) The direction of twist is opposite in each process.

(2) This twisting process is called LAYING the rope.

(3) When the strands are twisted to form the rope they are also turned individually in the direction of their original twist.

(4) The rope then resembles a coil-spring and the harder the twist the shorter and more elastic becomes the rope.

(5) When under strain much of the strength of the rope comes from the friction that is developed between the various parts.

Rope is made up of either 3 or 4 strands. The lay of the rope is left- or right-handed according to the direction of the twist of the strands in laying up the rope in the final twisting process.

The strands may be laid up round a central core.

There are three main types of rope.

(1) **Hawser-laid** rope is 3-stranded and generally laid up right-handed. It is the most common type in use.

4 stranded
right hand lay

(also known as
shroud laid)

Hawser
laid   3 stranded   Right hand   Left hand

(2) **Shroud-laid** rope is 4-stranded and laid up round a central core sometimes known as the heart.

(3) **Cable-laid** rope is made up by twisting together three hawser-laid ropes. It gives a very elastic rope useful for towing. Three lengths of left-handed lead line laid up into one length of right-handed cable laid rope and strongly whipped half-way along and at one end make a lovely 'tail' to practise splicing.

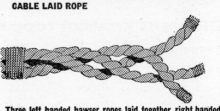

CABLE LAID ROPE

Three left handed hawser ropes laid together right handed

To improve the lasting quality of the rope it is often:

(1) Impregnated with oil when it is being made. This is known as OIL SPUN rope.

(2) TARRED as a finishing process.

Wire ropes

(1) Nearly all WIRE ROPE used at sea is 6-stranded. The strand wires are twisted to the left and it is laid up right-handed. Both the strands themselves and the whole rope may have a core or heart of jute, hemp or steel. The heart has a cushioning effect and a fibre heart absorbs the oils with which the rope may be dressed so that when the rope is stretched the oils are exuded and act as a lubricant.

Wire rope

Six stranded

(2) Each strand is made up of many wires. The greater the number of wires the more flexible is the finished rope. Standing rigging requires stiff wire and may have 7 or 19 wires in the strand. Wire rope used for running rigging must be more flexible and may have 12 or 30 wires to the strand. It is known as FLEXIBLE STEEL WIRE ROPE. Flexible wire rope always has a hemp heart and often hemp hearts in each strand in which case it is extra flexible.

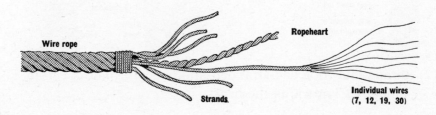

Wire rope

Ropeheart

Strands

Individual wires
(7, 12, 19, 30)

Example of how to describe wire rope
Wire rope made of 6 strands with 19 wires to each strand is described as 6/19.

A comparison of wire rope and cordage
 (1) The main difference in construction is that cordage is made of fibres of short length and the wire in the strands of wire rope are long lengths.
 (2) Wire rope is:
  much stronger. Size for size it is about ten times stronger than hemp;
  less elastic. It is not so good for towing and anchoring but is better for standing rigging and for parts of halyards;
  more difficult to handle. Greater care is needed to select the size of block through which it passes;
  more durable and does not absorb water.

Measuring ropes

 (1) Length: in fathoms.
 (2) Size:
  (i) Cordage—circumference in inches.
  (ii) Wire—manufacturers quote 'diameter in inches' but seamen still refer to 'circumference in inches'.
 (3) Strength:
  (i) CORDAGE, except coir rope.
  Breaking strain is $\frac{\text{circumference}^2}{3}$. Answer in tons.
  Occasional safe working load $=\frac{1}{2}$ breaking strain.
  Working load $=\frac{1}{6}$ breaking strain.
  (ii) WIRE
  Breaking strain $=$ circumference$^2 \times$ a constant $=$ answer in tons.
  The constant (e.g. flexible steel wire $\times 2$) varies according to the type of wire.
  Working load $=\frac{1}{6}$ of breaking strain (approximately).

Handling rope

There are three items of equipment for handling rope which you should always carry, preferably in a special pocket and secured with a lanyard as necessary.

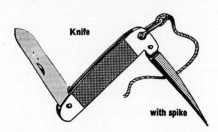

Knife

with spike

(1) A SEAMAN'S KNIFE. The blade should be rounded rather than pointed and kept sharp. It may be necessary to cut a rope quickly in an emergency. Keep the blade oiled to prevent it from rusting.

(2) A MARLINE-SPIKE for opening up rope, particularly wire for splicing.

(3) SAIL TWINE, PALM, NEEDLE and BEESWAX for whipping.

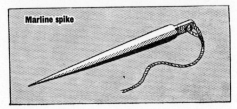

Marline spike

How to make and use knots, bends and hitches

KNOTS, BENDS and HITCHES are for fastening ropes to one another or to another object. They have to take strains continuously or in jerks, to be made easily and cast off quickly and without difficulty.

All knots, bends and hitches reduce the strength of a rope by about 50 per cent at the point where they are made.

Parts of a rope

The terms which describe the parts of a rope used in making knots, bends and hitches are:

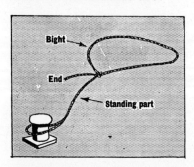

Bight

End

Standing part

BIGHT—the middle part of a length of rope or a loop of a rope.

END—the part of a rope which does no work. It is the part which is left over after the knot, bend or hitch is made.

STANDING PART—the part of the rope which does the work, i.e. the opposite part of a rope to the end.

Choosing the right knot, bend and hitch

To prevent a rope unreeving through an eye, block or fairlead use either an **overhand knot** or a **figure-of-eight.**

To join two ropes of equal size use a **reef knot.**

A reef knot is reliable and will not slip, jam, or come undone like a **granny.**

To join two ropes of unequal size use a **sheet bend** or a **double sheet bend.**

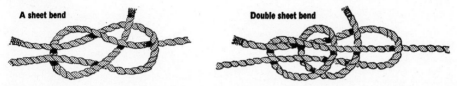

The round turn used in the double sheet bend makes it more secure and it takes a greater strain.

To take a strain and secure a rope to a ring, rail or spar use a **round turn** secured with a **half hitch** which is a temporary fastening or with **two half hitches** which makes the knot more secure and it will take a heavier load.

A **fisherman's bend** can also be used. It is more suitable for taking the strain of a jerking pull but may jam and is more difficult to cast off. It is better for a permanent fastening in which case the end should be stopped to the standing part, e.g. a boat's warp to her anchor.

To shorten a rope use a **sheepshank.**

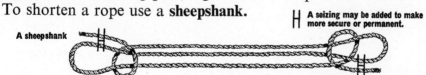

To secure a rope to a spar or pillar use a **timber hitch** or a **clove hitch.** Both these hitches will slip with a sideways pull.

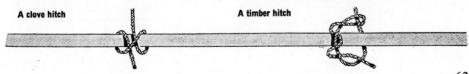

To secure a rope to a spar so that the rope will not slip sideways use a **timber hitch** and a **half hitch** or a **rolling hitch.**

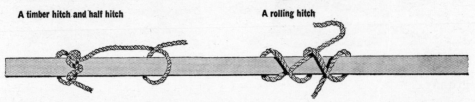

A timber hitch and half hitch   A rolling hitch

To make a large temporary eye in the end of a rope use a **bowline.**

A Bowline

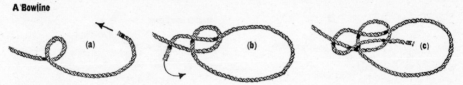

(a)   (b)   (c)

If the end of the rope is not available but only a bight use a **bowline on a bight.**

A BOWLINE ON A BIGHT

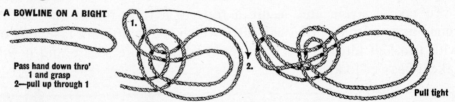

Pass hand down thro'
1 and grasp
2—pull up through 1

1.   2.   Pull tight

Finishing rope ends

WHIPPINGS, SPLICES and certain KNOTS are used to finish off the ends of wire rope and cordage to prevent the wires from springing apart and the fibre ropes from fraying.

To **whip** a rope is to bind and secure its end with twine. There are four common methods:

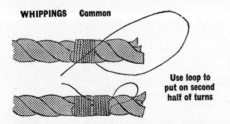

WHIPPINGS   Common

Use loop to
put on second
half of turns

Common whipping. This is easy to make and is reliable.

American

American whipping is similar to the common whipping except that the first end is left clear between the

The same but finish with a reef
knot in middle using both ends.

first and second group of turns and the two ends are then tied with a reef knot.

64

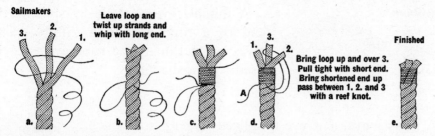

Sailmaker's whipping. This takes a little longer to make but it is the most secure and reliable whipping. It will not work adrift.

West country whipping. This is particularly useful to whip the bight or middle of a rope.

Pointing a rope is not difficult to do and provided a simple RON finish is used it is the perfect end for finishing a rope.

Splices are a more permanent method of finishing the ends of rope.

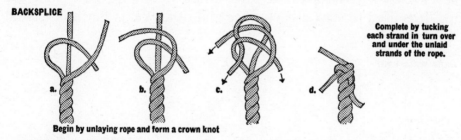

The **backsplice** has the disadvantage that it will not run through a block the correct size for the rope.

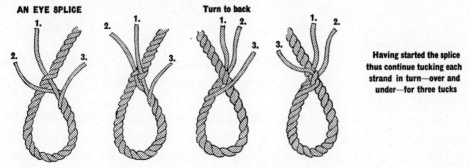

Thimble eye

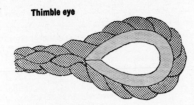

A **thimble eye** is made by splicing the end of a rope around a thimble. This gives protection if the rope eye is to be used with a shackle.

A **hawser eye.** The eye is spliced larger than the thimble which is then secured and fitted with a seizing. It has the advantage that if the thimble is damaged it can be replaced without making a new eye splice.

Hawser eye

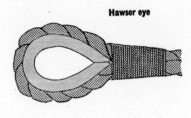

Soft eye.

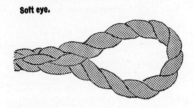

A **soft eye** is used if there is no chafing in the eye from a metal part. It can be converted to a hawser eye if required.

Knots

The CROWN KNOT leaves the three strands pointing back along the rope. It is used to start a backsplice and other knots but it is seldom used on its own.

THE WALL KNOT

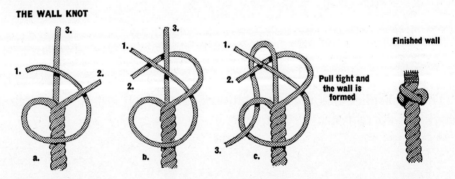

The WALL KNOT is a crown knot upside down. If the crown knot or wall knot are used on their own the strands should be whipped to the rope.

The CROWN AND WALL. The crown is made first and the wall underneath.

The WALL AND CROWN is made in the reverse order and position.

66

Stowing ropes

For stowing ropes are COILED, FLAKED or CHEESED.

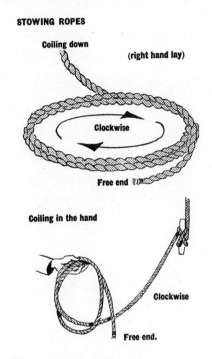

STOWING ROPES

Coiling down

(right hand lay)

Clockwise

Free end

Coiling in the hand

Clockwise

Free end.

COILING DOWN or in the hand avoids twists, turns and kinks particularly when a rope has to run through a block or sheave.

(1) When coiling the free end is coiled last.

(2) The part of the rope left uncoiled is given one turn each time a loop is formed in the coil to prevent kinking.

(3) Rope with a right hand lay is coiled down right handed, that is, clockwise, and vice versa.

(4) When the coil is finished the free end is on top. If it is required to run out turn it over to bring the standing part on top.

(5) A coil of small line can be made up in the hand.

If a rope is required to run out very quickly it is FLAKED DOWN, particularly when the space where the rope is to be stowed is long

Flaking down

and narrow. The turn at the end is laid over the previous turn to prevent it from catching up.

CHEESING DOWN is used to make a neat stow of a fairly short end. Never use this method when a rope has to run quickly through a block.

Left hand lay

Flemish Coil

Cheesed down

Free end

Throwing a heaving line

A HEAVING LINE is a light flexible line, for example, 15 fathoms of 1 inch fibre rope, used to pass a warp or heavy rope from ship to ship, or ship to shore. It is only strong enough to take the strain of the weight of the warp. One end may be whipped or have a backsplice and the other end may have a heaving line knot such as a wall and crown knot to give it some weight.

For use it should be wetted and made up into two coils—about two-thirds of the rope held in the left hand, about one-third in the right hand for throwing, and the whole ready to run out easily. The end of the left-hand coil should be made fast. The right-hand coil is thrown by swinging the arm and body.

Belaying

To BELAY a rope is to make fast or secure a rope which is under strain, so that it cannot slip but can be cast off quickly and easily.

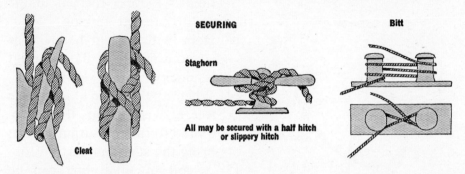

SECURING

Bitt

Staghorn

Cleat

All may be secured with a half hitch or slippery hitch

A CLEAT, a STAGHORN or a BOLLARD is a fitting designed for this purpose. The rope is made fast by taking a sufficient number of turns round the fitting so that it holds by friction.

To secure to a cleat or staghorn first take a round turn and complete with several figure-of-eight turns.

Beware when completing with a half hitch because this may jam if the rope becomes wet. Jamming belays are almost always due to the besetting sin of the British seaman— choosing gear that is too small. A jam on a really big enough cleat is extremely rare and a hitched belay is safer than an open one.

The diagram shows how to hang a coil on to a fitting designed for belaying.

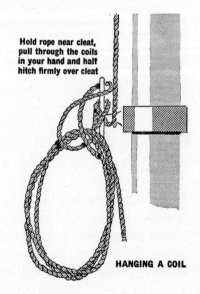

Hold rope near cleat, pull through the coils in your hand and half hitch firmly over cleat

HANGING A COIL

68

Some more splices

The backsplice and eyesplice are used for finishing off the end of a rope. Two ends of a rope or ropes may be joined permanently by making a SHORT SPLICE or a LONG SPLICE.

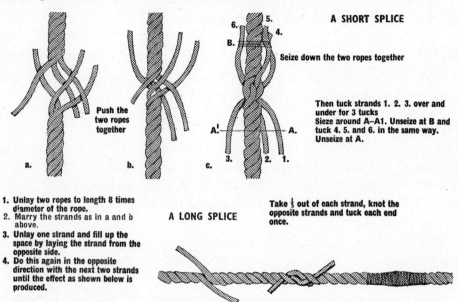

A SHORT SPLICE

Seize down the two ropes together

Push the two ropes together

Then tuck strands 1. 2. 3. over and under for 3 tucks
Sieze around A–A1. Unseize at B and tuck 4. 5. and 6. in the same way.
Unseize at A.

a.   b.   c.

1. Unlay two ropes to length 8 times diameter of the rope.
2. Marry the strands as in a and b above.
3. Unlay one strand and fill up the space by laying the strand from the opposite side.
4. Do this again in the opposite direction with the next two strands until the effect as shown below is produced.

A LONG SPLICE

Take ⅓ out of each strand, knot the opposite strands and tuck each end once.

Both are equally reliable. The short splice is quicker and easier to make but in making it the rope is thickened and it will not pass through a block of the correct size, whereas the long splice will pass through the block.

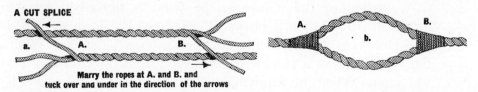

A CUT SPLICE

a.   A.   B.

Marry the ropes at A. and B. and tuck over and under in the direction of the arrows

A.   B.   b.

Two ropes may be joined and a loop or eye formed at the join by making a CUT SPLICE.

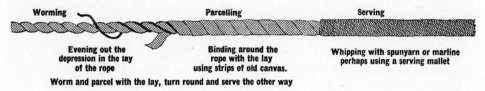

Worming   Parcelling   Serving

Evening out the depression in the lay of the rope

Binding around the rope with the lay using strips of old canvas.

Whipping with spunyarn or marline perhaps using a serving mallet

Worm and parcel with the lay, turn round and serve the other way

To protect a rope where a splice has been made or for any other reason it is WORMED, PARCELLED and SERVED.

8. How a Boat Sails

Three things help each other to make a boat sail: the wind, the water and the way they both act on the boat.

Wind

If the sails are the heart of a boat, the wind is her life-blood. Study the wind from two aspects, DIRECTION and STRENGTH.

Direction of wind

The direction of the wind is shown by a burgee or by a racing flag hoisted to the top of the mast. If there is no burgee, tie small pieces of cotton to the shrouds as a substitute. An experienced sailor rarely needs a burgee because he can tell where the wind is coming from by feeling it on his face.

The direction of the wind is described in three different ways in relation to (1) the compass, (2) the boat, and (3) the shore.

(1) A COMPASS is a small device to enable us to detect the direction of north. It consists of a needle or pointer one end of which is attracted to magnetic north.

According to the compass, the wind is described by the direction from which it blows. Winds from the west are called WESTERLIES, and from the north-east, NOR'EASTERS. When the wind shifts in a clockwise direction round the compass it is VEERING. When the wind changes direction anti-clockwise it is BACKING. A backing wind often foretells a blow.

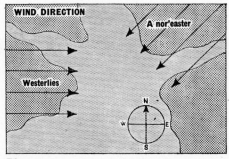

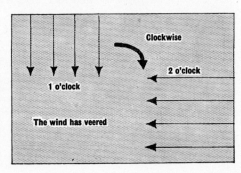

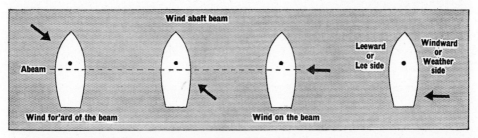

(2) (*a*) In relation to the boat the wind is either for'ard of the beam, on the beam, or aft of the beam.

(*b*) The fore-and-aft line divides the boat into two halves, and the side from which the wind blows is known as the WIND-WARD or WEATHER SIDE and the side away from the wind is the LEEWARD or LEE SIDE.

(3) If the wind is blowing on to the shore it is an ON-SHORE wind, and if it is blowing off the shore it is an OFF-SHORE wind. The shore on to which it is blowing is a LEE SHORE and the shore from which it is blowing is a WEATHER SHORE.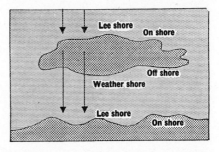

There is a **true wind** and an **apparent wind.** The burgee shows the **true wind** when the boat is stationary. When she is moving she is setting up another wind by her movement. The burgee then indicates the combined direction of the true wind and the movement of the boat. This is the APPARENT WIND. It is the direction of the apparent wind which is important to the sailor when handling his boat.

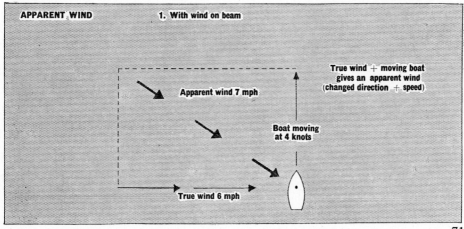

If a boat is sailing along with the wind the effect is to reduce its strength. This is an important point because there has been many an accident when a boat has turned into a wind that is really much stronger than seemed to her skipper while she was running with it.

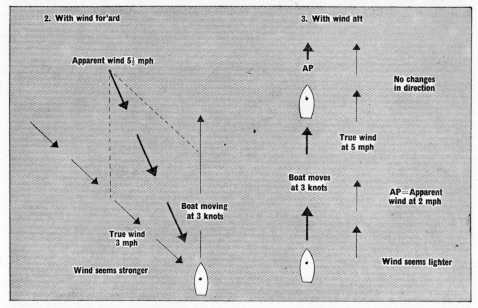

Motto: judge the wind's strength by the appearance of the water and not by its feel on your face. With the wind forward the wind strength is increased.

Strength of wind

The burgee not only shows the direction of the wind but also its strength. In light airs it will flutter gently and in a fresh breeze it will blow straight out. Always watch the strength of the wind which can change quite suddenly from a calm to a gale. In a calm the air is still, the burgee drops, the water looks like glass and smoke rises vertically. In a gale the speed of the wind is more than 30 miles an hour, white foam blows in flecks from the heavy seas and ashore the trees will be swaying in the wind. On the strength of the wind will depend whether or not you sail, whether you carry full sail or reef and, finally, whether you will reach your destination.

The **Beaufort scale** by which meteorologists describe the wind strength is an accepted guide. It is worth learning this and relating it to your own local knowledge and experience. The Table is based on information provided in *The Weather Map* (H.M.S.O.).

The Beaufort Scale of Wind

NO	SPEED IN M.P.H.	NAME	SIGNS USEFUL TO SMALL BOAT SAILORS	
0	Less than 1	Calm	1 Smoke rises vertically 2 Sea like a mirror	**Sails will not fill.** Drifting, oars and ground tackle needed
1	3	Light air	1 Smoke drifts 2 Ripples on the water	**Dinghies can sail.** Fishing smack just has steerage way —sails just full
2	4–7	Light breeze	1 Leaves rustle—wind felt on face 2 Small wavelets—crests do not break	**Fair breeze for small boat sailors at sea.** Fishing smacks' sails fill and they do 1–2 knots. Beware of adverse tide if beating.
3	8–12	Gentle breeze	1 Wind extends light flag 2 Large wavelets—many crests break—scattered white horses	**Ideal breeze for small boats at sea. All sit to windward.** Fishing smacks begin to heel and sail at 3–4 knots
4	13–18	Moderate breeze	1 Raises dust and loose paper ashore 2 Small waves. Frequent white horses	**All dinghies reef. Advisable not to venture outside harbour or estuary.** Good working breeze for smacks
5	19–24	Fresh breeze	1 Wavelets with crests begin to form on inland waters 2 Moderate waves—white horses and spray at sea	**All dinghies fully reefed and require sitting out. Only sail in sheltered water and only if very experienced.** Smacks shorten sail or reef.
6	25–31	Strong breeze	1 Whistling heard in telegraph wire and rigging wires 2 Large waves — white foam crests spray at sea	**No small boats out.** Smacks have mainsail fully reefed and care required when fishing and they may lie to at sea
7	32–38	Near gale	1 Sea heaps up and is very broken—waves break 2 Ashore—whole trees in motion	**No small boats out.** Smacks stay in harbour, those at sea 'heave to'

Water

Water affects a sailing-boat in three ways:

(1) It supports the boat on or near its surface. A boat which sails through the water with a good deal of hull below the surface has

73

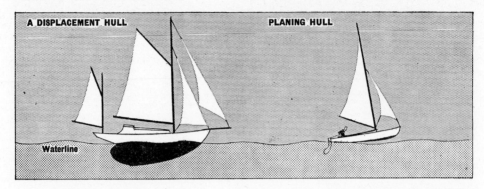

a DISPLACEMENT HULL because the hull displaces a lot of water. Deep keel boats displace more water than boats with shallow, flat hulls which travel fast and plane on the surface of the water, and are known as PLANING HULLS.

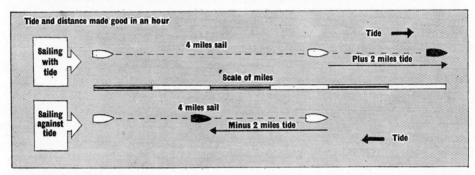

(2) Sea-water is tidal and the tides affect the passage of a boat. Try to work the tides to your advantage. A boat making 4 knots through the water with a supporting tide running at 2 knots will reach her destination in a third of the time that she would do against the tide.

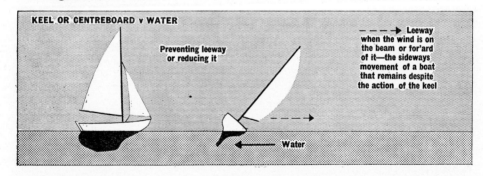

(3) Water prevents the boat from being blown sideways by setting up a resistance to the keel or centre-board.

74

Making a passage—three points of sailing

Imagine you are going to sail clockwise round the island. The passage will be shown in a diagram in which the boat and her sails will look like this. This is also the key to further illustration in the following chapters.

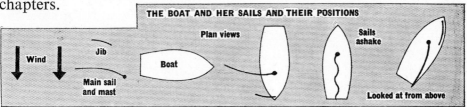

THE BOAT AND HER SAILS AND THEIR POSITIONS

Plan views — Sails ashake

Wind — Jib — Boat — Main sail and mast — Looked at from above

Imagine that the wind will continue to blow steadily from the west and will not change direction. *Pickle Point* is the anchorage from which you set out and to which you return. To make this passage you have to sail in three different directions. Each direction is a leg of the passage and represents the three different points of sailing, RUNNING, REACHING and BEATING.

The number of legs in a passage depends on the distance to be sailed and the number of times it is necessary to change course in relation to the direction of the wind.

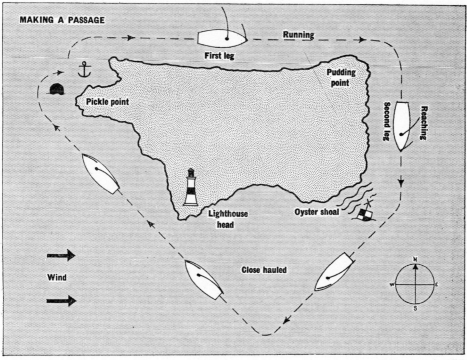

MAKING A PASSAGE

Running

First leg

Pudding point

Pickle point

Second leg

Reaching

Lighthouse head

Oyster shoal

Close hauled

Wind

First leg from Pickle Point to Pudding Point—Running

You are sailing east along the north shore with the wind aft, i.e. behind you. Your point of sailing is RUNNING BEFORE THE WIND or RUNNING WITH THE WIND AFT. The expression sailing OFF THE WIND is also used. The wind blows you along like a leaf in a country lane. If the sails were lowered the wind would still blow the the boat along but she would move more slowly.

Second leg from Pudding Point to Oyster Shoal—Reaching

You are sailing towards the south along the east shore with the wind on the beam coming across the starboard side of your boat. Your point of sailing is REACHING, with the wind free, or ON A REACH. This cross wind is sometimes called a SOLDIER'S WIND because going either way it is easy enough for even a soldier to manage.

Why isn't the boat blown sideways? The **orange pip theory** is a simple explanation which does not give the complete answer but helps to build up a picture of what happens. Take an orange pip and squeeze it between your forefinger and thumb. The pip will jump forwards according to the amount of pressure used.

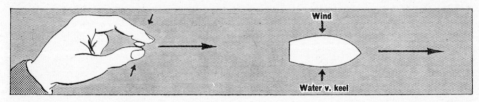

Apply this to a sailing boat with the wind on the beam. The wind blows across the windward side of the boat and presses on the sails which pass on the pressure to the hull. The boat will be blown sideways if this pressure is not resisted. Resistance is offered by the pressure of the water on the underwater surface of the boat's hull in the opposite direction, and is increased by the boat's keel or centreboard. If your forefinger represents the pressure of the wind on the sails and your thumb the pressure of the water on the hull this will explain partly why the boat moves like the orange pip.

Third leg from Oyster Shoal to Pickle Point—Beating to windward

You are sailing west along the south shore until you reach LIGHTHOUSE HEAD. The true wind is coming from straight ahead and is called a headwind. If you point the boat dead into the wind the sails merely shake and flap and they fail to capture the force of the wind.

76

The boat is HEAD TO WIND or IN IRONS, and is eventually blown backwards. You cannot sail directly into the true wind and you have to steer the boat on another course as close as possible to the direction of the wind. The nearest your boat will sail is on a course which is at an angle of about 45 degrees to the true wind.

Your point of sailing is BEATING TO WINDWARD or CLOSE-HAULED. The sails are hauled close inboard with the end of the boom over the boat's quarter. The expression SAILING ON THE WIND is also used and the course is to windward.

To reach LIGHTHOUSE HEAD you can either sail a series of short courses, nearly zigzag, or two long boards. A leg or course when beating to windward is described as a BOARD or TACK. The decision whether you are likely to reach your objective safely and more quickly by a greater number of short tacks or fewer long tacks depends on local conditions, e.g. weather, state of the sea, and tide.

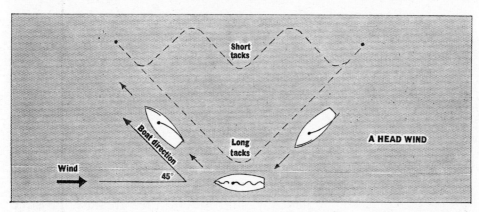

When you have reached LIGHTHOUSE HEAD, your course for PICKLE POINT lies north-west and is at an angle of about 45 degrees to the true wind. The wind comes from for'ard over the port bow and you are still sailing to windward. There is no need to tack or sail zigzag for you can now FETCH the anchorage in one long tack or board, and you are still on the same point of sailing, i.e. close-hauled without another tack.

Position of the sails
On each of the three legs the boat is on a different point of sailing: (1) running, with the wind aft or nearly aft; (2) reaching, with the wind on the side of the boat; and (3) close-hauled, pointing as close into the wind as the boat can sail.

77

The sails are set on the lee side of the boat and the headsails are roughly in line with the mainsail, the position of the sails depends on the point of sailing.

The sails are adjusted by HAULING IN and PAYING OUT the sheets according to the point of sailing.

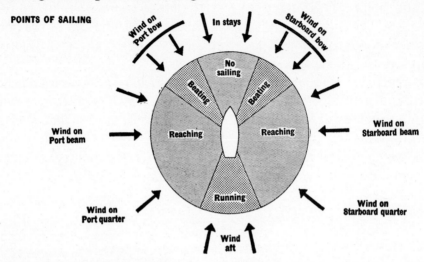

POINTS OF SAILING

(1) Running

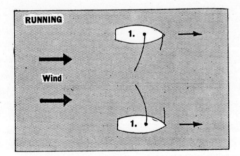

The wind blows across the port or starboard quarter or from dead aft. The mainsail is sheeted right off so that the boom is nearly at right angles to the following wind and offers the greatest possible area to it.

(2) Reaching, with the wind free

This means the boat is free to sail closer to the wind or with the wind further aft as the helmsman requires. If the wind blows from for'ard of the beam the boat is on a CLOSE or FINE REACH. If it blows from well aft of the beam the boat is on a BROAD REACH.

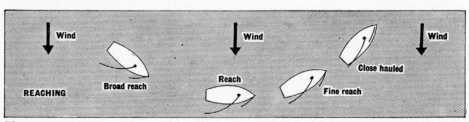

On a close reach the sails are freed from the close-hauled position by easing or paying out the sheets. On a broad reach the sheets are eased still further until the boom is rather more than half-way out.

(3) Beating to windward or close-hauled

The mainsail is sheeted home so that the outer end of the boom is close inboard over or near the boat's quarter, and the headsail is sheeted hard in.

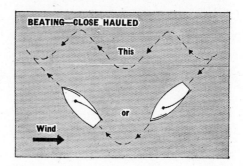

Port and Starboard Tacks

On all points of sailing the wind comes from, and over, one side of the boat—the opposite side from the boom and sails.

(1) If the wind is on the starboard side (from for'ard, on the beam, or aft) the boat is sailing on the **starboard tack.**

(2) If the wind is on the port side (for'ard, abeam or aft) the boat is sailing on the **port tack.**

You may beat, reach or run on either the starboard or port tack.

Ask yourself the question, 'On which side is the wind?' The answer tells you what tack you are on—port or starboard.

9. Tides

Ebb and Flow

There are two main features about tides. First the regular RISE and FALL of the waters of the sea and second, in conjuction with this, the FLOW and EBB of water in a harbour or along a shore.

The rising tide which flows into the shore is the FLOOD and the falling tide which recedes or runs back from the shore is the EBB. Between the flood and the ebb there is a period of SLACK WATER.

It is dangerous to generalize because local conditions vary but the following is a guide to the way in which tides ebb and flow.

Each day, i.e. approximately every 24 hours, there are two **High Tides** with an interval of 12 hours 25 minutes in between, so that *high tides occur about 50 minutes later every day.*

The tide rises or flows for about 6 hours and falls or ebbs for about 6 hours and there is a period of 25 minutes slack water in between.

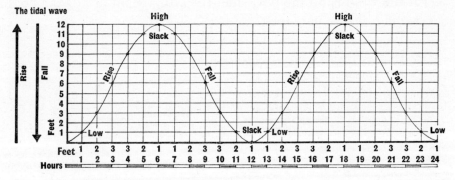

The tide takes about 6 hours to rise and it is slow to start, speeds up at about half flood and then slows down again. If there were a 12-foot rise of tide the rise each hour would be 1 foot, 2 feet, 3 feet, 3 feet, 2 feet, 1 foot. The speed of the tidal current roughly corresponds to this both on ebb and flow.

Rise and fall speed and ebb and flow speed proportion or rate
PROPORTION OR RATE

Slack 1	2	3	3	2	1	Slack (25 minutes)
1st hr	2nd hr	3rd hr	4th hr	5th hr	6th hr	

There are many local variations in tidal conditions and times for ebb and flow. Sometimes the tides lag behind their forecast time because winds hold them up. At other times they are early.

80

Spring and Neaps

Tides are caused by the attraction that the sun and moon have for the waters of the earth.

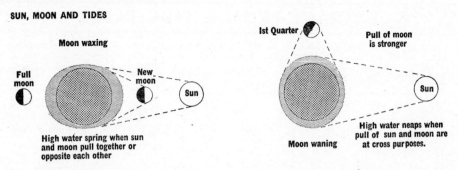

SUN, MOON AND TIDES

Moon waxing

Full moon

New moon

Sun

High water spring when sun and moon pull together or opposite each other

1st Quarter

Pull of moon is stronger

Sun

Moon waning

High water neaps when pull of sun and moon are at cross purposes.

N.B. 1. Earth around sun once a year   2. Moon around Earth 13 times a year

The **Spring Tides** or **Springs** are the **High Tides** which occur twice in 29 days. The Spring Tides occur at full moon when the sun and moon pull against each other and at new moon when the sun and moon pull together. There is a regular time-lag due to geographic position in the way the Spring Tides occur after the full and new moons. They are often spread over a period of two or three days. One tide is forecast to be higher than the others but perhaps by only a few inches and it may occur during the hours of darkness. Two Springs occur in 24 hours, i.e. all tides for say a couple of days are Spring Tides with little difference between them.

High water springs
High water neaps

Low water neaps
Low water springs

1. High water is higher
2. Low water is lower at springs
3. Spring tides run faster

The **Neap Tides** are the **lower High Tides** which occur in between the Spring Tides. At Neaps the High Tides are less high than at Springs and the Low Tides are less low. A difference in the rise and fall of from 6 to 12 feet is quite common between Springs and Neaps. When the tides are increasing from the Neap to the Spring Tides they are said to be MAKING. When the tides are decreasing from the Spring Tides to the Neap Tides they are said to be TAKING OFF.

HIGH WATER FULL AND CHANGE i.e. Springs always occurs at the same time or hour in any one harbour or point around the coastline. From knowing the time of high tide on any day in your harbour you can tell whether the tides are making or taking off.

At Blakeney, HWF and C is at approximately 7 p.m. When high water is between 12 noon and 7 p.m. the tides are making. When high water is between 7 a.m. and 12 noon they are taking off.

EXTRACT FROM A TIDE TABLE

APRIL		MORNING		AFTERNOON			MOON
DATE	DAY	HOUR MINUTES	DEPTH	HOUR MINUTES	DEPTH		
9	Th	7.5	28 ft 0	7.14	28 ft 1	} SPRINGS	8th April
10	F	7.35	28 0	7.46	27 11		New Moon
11	S	8.3	27 9	8.18	27 5		4.29 a.m.
12	S	8.33	27 1	8.51	26 6	Taking off	
13	M	9.2	26 3	9.25	25 5		
14	T	9.33	25 2	10.5	24 3		16th April
15	W	10.11	24 0	10.53	23 1		1st Quarter
16	Th	11.2	23 1	11.59	22 3		8.22 a.m.
17	F	—	—	12.10	22 6	} Neaps	
18	S	1.23	22 5	1.34	23 0		23rd April
19	S	2.39	23 8	2.49	24 6		Full Moon
20	M	3.41	25 7	3.50	26 6	Making	6.13 a.m.
21	T	4.33	27 5	4.43	28 5		
22	W	5.22	29 1	5.34	29 9		
23	Th	6.7	30 3	6.23	30 8	} SPRINGS	29th April
24	F	6.53	30 7	7.10	30 9		Last Quarter
25	S	7.35	29 1	7.55	30 5		9.38 a.m.

N B
1   Spring Tides—7 a.m. and 7 p.m. (approx).
2   Neap Tides—Mid-day tides (at this port).
3   Spring Tides at New Moon and Full Moon.
4   Table gives TIME and the Height of HIGH WATER above LOW WATER at Springs.

How tides affect small boat sailors

Rise and fall of tides and beaching

If you come on to a hard or a beach for repairs or scrubbing the boat's bottom be sure the tides are making so that you have enough water to get off the next day or the day after.

If the tides are taking off make sure you beach your boat at half tide so that she will float off when you want her.

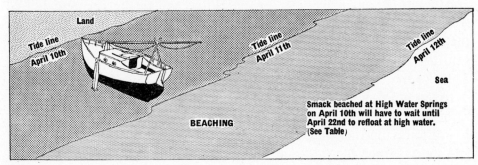

Land

Tide line April 10th

Tide line April 11th

Tide line April 12th

Sea

Smack beached at High Water Springs on April 10th will have to wait until April 22nd to refloat at high water. (See Table)

BEACHING

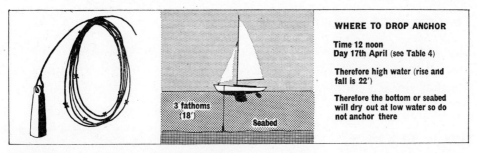

WHERE TO DROP ANCHOR

Time 12 noon
Day 17th April (see Table 4)

Therefore high water (rise and fall is 22')

Therefore the bottom or seabed will dry out at low water so do not anchor there

3 fathoms (18')

Seabed

Choosing an anchorage or mooring

When choosing a position in which to anchor, check the depth with a LEAD LINE, particularly if she is a keel boat. Look at the tide tables for the rise and fall and state of the tide to make sure she will still be afloat at low water.

When selecting a place for putting down moorings try to ensure that the boat will still be afloat at low water in whichever direction she may lie.

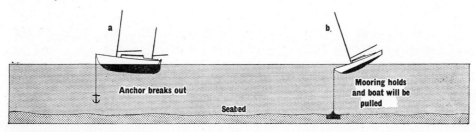

a

b.

Anchor breaks out

Mooring holds and boat will be pulled

Seabed

Paying out the chain

If the anchor rope or chain is too short the anchor will drag at high water.

If the length of riding scope on a mooring is too short the boat may be pulled under at high water and sink.

Jetty

Tied up on too short painter. Boat will swamp.

Tying-up

It is important to consider the state of the tide to decide how much painter is required when tying up the dinghy to a jetty or post.

Making a passage

As a general principle it is wiser not to make a passage in shallow water on a falling tide.

83

The flow of water or current

The speed of the current of a flow of water may add or subtract 2 or 3 knots to the rate at which the boat is sailing, depending on whether she is sailing with or against the tide.

How to work tides

(1) Sail out of an estuary with the ebb and return on the flood.

(2) Sail up a river going inland on the flood and return to the harbour near the coast on the ebb.

(3) When making a coastal passage sail out of the estuary on the ebb. Local conditions vary but you will need to judge at what state of the ebb it is best to start sailing out of the estuary. For example, if you are sailing on the East Coast of the British Isles and if you want to sail up the main flood stream, go out on the last of the ebb and catch the first of the new flood to help you on your way. If you are planning to sail down the main ebb stream—on the East Coast that would be northwards—sail out of the estuary on the first of the ebb so that you can carry it with you for as long as possible.

(4) If there is a forecast of a dying wind try to plan your sail so that the tide will be with you at the end of the day. Avoid returning with the wind and the tide against you. If this is impossible do a test before sailing out too far to see what progress the boat will make against both wind and tide.

(5) Study local conditions to find out where the tide ebbs and flows most strongly, where there are eddy currents and where there is slacker water.

Effect of ebb and flow on the state of the water

(1) With the wind against the tide the surface of the water becomes broken.

(2) With wind and tide together the surface of the water is smoother.

(3) An on-shore wind, that is, a wind from seaward, will build up bigger seas.

(4) If there is an off-shore wind, that is, a wind blowing from the land, the surface of the water is smoother.

Measuring at sea

(1) The **depth** of water is measured in FATHOMS.
1 fathom=6 feet.
Measurement of the depth of water is referred to as SOUND-INGS.

(2) **Distance.** A NAUTICAL or SEA MILE=6080 feet.
A CABLE=$\frac{1}{10}$ of 1 sea mile, i.e. 200 yards approximately, or 100 fathoms.

(3) **Speed** of water or of a boat is measured in KNOTS.
1 knot=1 nautical, sea or geographical mile per hour.
A knot is therefore a speed.

LEAD-LINE MARKS

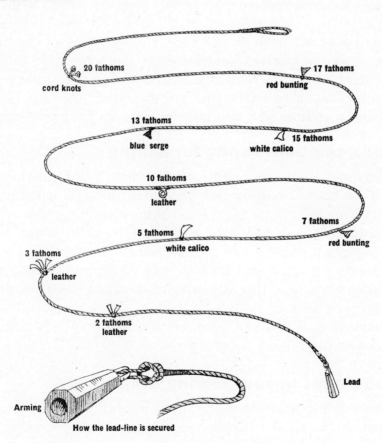

20 fathoms

cord knots

17 fathoms

red bunting

13 fathoms

blue serge

15 fathoms

white calico

10 fathoms

leather

7 fathoms

5 fathoms

white calico

red bunting

3 fathoms

leather

2 fathoms
leather

Lead

Arming

How the lead-line is secured

85

There are many ways of learning to sail. You may be asked to crew in someone else's boat. You will learn the crew's job first under the direction of the helmsman or skipper. You will be able to watch the practised hand at the helm. The time will come when the helmsman will need a rest and if he has sufficient confidence in you he will ask you to steer the boat. This is a good method of learning because the experienced helmsman is on the spot and can tell you or show you what to do. By the time the helmsman wants to hand over, the boat is normally in open water and you will have plenty of sea-room. In this way you should become thoroughly competent in straightforward sailing.

Taking over the helm in open water is only part of the business. Everyone who skippers a boat must get the boat ready for sailing, and he must know how to use the wind and the tide to sail away from moorings. This chapter tells you how to prepare the boat for sailing and the next chapter tells you how to get away from moorings.

Getting the boat ready for sailing

You may find yourselves in any one of at least three situations:
  (1) Your boat, a half-decked Bermudan sloop, is lying at anchor and you have to go afloat in a rowing dinghy.
  (2) You keep your boat ashore in a dinghy park or trail it by car to a place where it can be launched.
  (3) Yours is a cruising yacht with sleeping accommodation and you sleep aboard, so that you are already afloat when you decide to go for a sail.

Whichever it is you will need a cockpit drill so that nothing important gets forgotten.

Going afloat in your rowing dinghy

To get to sailing boats on moorings or at anchor a TENDER is used. In most cases this is a small open rowing boat of between 8 and 12 feet long which is pulled by OARS that are placed in CRUTCHES or ROWLOCKS.

86

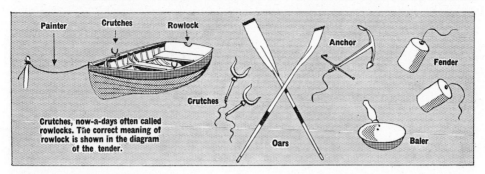

Crutches, now-a-days often called rowlocks. The correct meaning of rowlock is shown in the diagram of the tender.

The dinghy will have a PAINTER attached to the stem. This is a rope for securing the dinghy in-shore and for tying it up to the buoy when it is left on the mooring.

Before launching your dinghy check that you have oars, rowlocks, bailer and an anchor. Make sure the painter is attached to the stem of the dinghy.

Getting into the dinghy

When the dinghy is afloat step into the middle and sit down on the centre THWART. The thwarts are the planks which run across the dinghy from side to side to form seats. There are usually three thwarts, one placed for'ard, one in the centre, and one aft.

It is important to TRIM the boat so that she sits evenly in the water.

The crutches can normally be placed in two positions for rowing either from the centre thwart or from the for'ard thwart.

If you are alone, row from the centre thwart. If you are going to carry one other person load your passenger aft. Go for'ard and row from the for'ard thwart. If you are carrying several other people, remain on the centre thwart. Load one person aft, then one for'ard, then one aft in that order.

Leaving the jetty

Move off from the leeward side of the jetty or slipway so that the wind will help to blow you away.

Start rowing against the tide to test its strength and your ability to pull the boat against the tide in case you have to row back from your mooring under these conditions.

To know the effect of the tide is one of the most important points in handling a rowing dinghy in a crowded anchorage.

Aim to pass other boats just astern rather than cut close across their bows. Look out for mooring ropes which may hold you up.

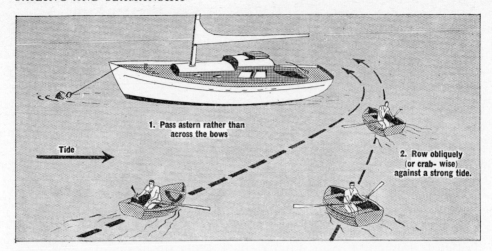

1. Pass astern rather than across the bows

Tide

2. Row obliquely (or crab- wise) against a strong tide.

To make a direct crossing of an anchorage with a strong tide running it may be necessary to point the boat obliquely up tide, that is, into the tide, for the crossing.

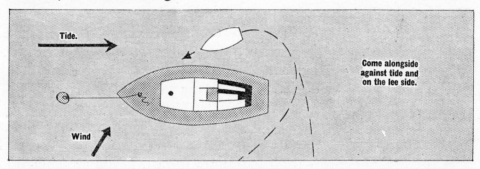

Tide.

Wind

Come alongside against tide and on the lee side.

The boat on its moorings should be lying with her bows pointing into the oncoming tide. If you approach the moored vessel from aft you will also be pointing into the tide which will act as a brake. Come alongside the moored vessel on the lee side which is most sheltered from the wind. In rough weather the water will be smoother.

If you try to come alongside with the tide and possibly with the wind behind you, it will be difficult to take way off as you come up to the moored vessel. You will require great physical force to hang on and you may be swept past or find yourself in collision with another boat.

Ship one oar and make your dinghy fast by passing the painter round a shroud or making fast to a cleat on the deck. Make fast as early as possible and if your boat has no permanent fender put out the fenders from your dinghy. Then go aboard and unload your dinghy in the reverse order.

A 12-point plan for getting the boat ready

(1) Check the things you are taking aboard before you leave the shore

Your personal clothing. As it is always colder when sailing than it is ashore, you will need:

Protection from cold, wind and spray

A woollen cap.
Heavy seaman-type jersey.
Canvas windproof smock, if you have one.
Canvas shorts or trousers. Girls will find skirts troublesome.
Light canvas shoes with non-slip rubber or rope soles.
(Loose layers of windproof clothing trap pockets of air and help to keep out the cold, so does a string vest.)

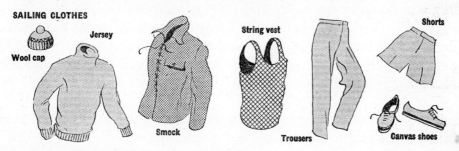

Protection from rough weather and rain

For a day's cruise take afloat all you need for rough weather sailing although the day may be warm and the weather calm when you set out. If you are racing for a couple of hours then you will not want to be overburdened with clothing. Be content to be 'wet below the waist and dry above it'.

Take: Oilskin smock or overcoat.
Oilskin shorts or over-trousers.
Sou'wester.
Change of clothing.

Protection if you go overboard

Even if you are a strong swimmer, it is a duty you owe to yourself and your crew to wear life-jackets.

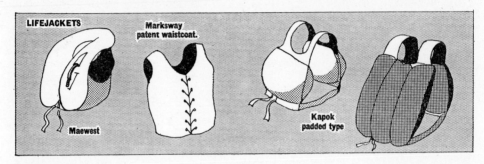

Avoid wearing sea boots because if you go overboard they will drag you down in the water and keep you down.

Avoid dark glasses because the spray and motion of the boat make them less useful than they might be on land. Unless you are used to glasses, they may dull the feel of the wind on your face and you will miss the subtle shifting of the wind.

Sail bags and all other gear kept ashore. See that you have all your sails, burgee and rowlocks.

The experienced sailor carries aboard a small canvas bag called a DITTY BAG with the following:

A sharp knife.

Marline-spike.

A pair of pliers or mole-type grip.

A few fathoms of lacing line sometimes called Hambro line or codline (say hemp $\frac{3}{8}$ in. circumference).

A sailmaker's palm and needle.

A few feet of sail canvas.

Wax.

A jar of grease.

Two or three small shackles.

A short length of seizing wire.

Twine.

A spare boat bung.

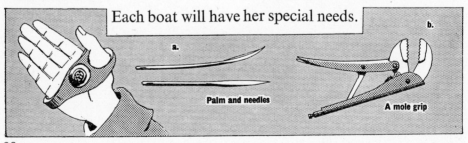

Each boat will have her special needs.

Palm and needles

A mole grip

(2) Row out to your boat on her mooring and make the dinghy fast
After you have made the dinghy fast unload it with care and without haste.

(3) See your sailing boat is dry inside
If your boat has been left on its moorings, there is bound to be some water in the bilges. This means wet feet and discomfort when sailing. Bilge water adds extra weight and shifting ballast to the boat. This can be a positive danger when sailing because the water will flow to

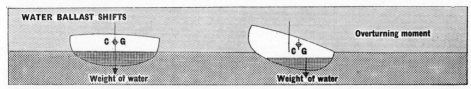

the low side of the boat and will increase the heel to leeward. Dry the inside of your boat with either a conventional metal baler and sponge or one of the new rubber balers. If the boat is equipped with a hand-pump this will speed up the job, and if she has a canvas boat cover pumping or drying out may be unnecessary.

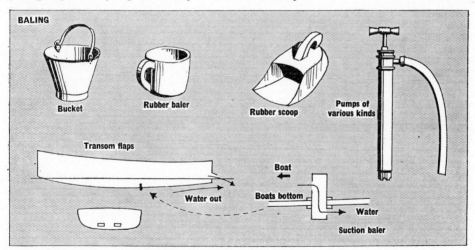

(4) Check that all movable gear is on board
Make sure the dinghy has been cleared of all the gear you intend to take with you. Check all other movable gear is on board:

Oars or paddles.	Sail battens.	Boat-hook.
Baler.	Spare ropes.	Anchor and warp.

If you are made fast to a mooring buoy you must still carry an anchor in order to drop anchor away from home.

(5) Hoist the burgee
Attach the burgee to the halyard.

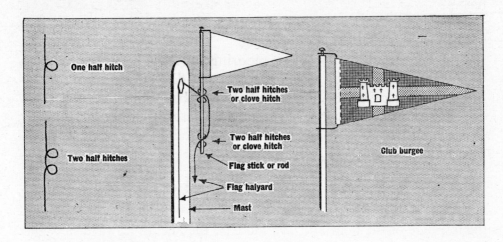

The burgee is shaped like an isosceles triangle. The colour and design may belong to a club or be personal to the owner. This burgee is used when cruising or at any time when you are not racing and is flown from the masthead.

The racing flag is rectangular in shape and can be of any colour and design. It tells the other craft that the boat is racing and should not be used for any other purpose.

(6) Check your standing rigging
If lanyard lines are in use and they are dry, wet them thoroughly to tighten up the rigging and check them for wear. Check that shackles are secure. If necessary tighten or loosen rigging or bottlescrews.

(7) Check your running rigging
It is particularly important to see that halyards are not twisted or tangled. It is too late to untangle your halyards when you have cast off your mooring and find you cannot hoist your jib or mainsail. Make sure that the jib sheets are attached to the jib, brought through the fairleads on the deck and a figure-of-eight or stopper knot tied at the ends. In particular see that the mainsheet is ready for use, without any tangles or kinks to prevent it from running through its blocks. Make sure it has a stopper knot at the end.

(8) Check centre-board, rudder and tiller

Centre-board. Hard mud, gravel, or a pebble may jam in the centre-board case and prevent the centre-board from moving up and down. It will only take two minutes to test this by lowering the centre-board. If you do not discover the centre-board is stuck until you are under way, there will be trouble because a boat will not go to windward without the centre-board and gets out of control.

If there is sufficient depth of water, lower the centre-board fully and leave it ready to sail away.

Rudder. Check the rudder is in position and undamaged. If it is a drop rudder, lower it and leave ready to sail away.

Tiller. Ship the tiller, i.e. put in position and secure. If it has an extension see that it works.

(9) Bend on the sails properly

It is important to do this properly because it is very easy to get a twist in a jib or to hoist it upside-down. It is impossible to put this right without lowering the sail. To prevent this happening, especially at night, remember that the bolt rope at the luff of sails is always sewn on the port side. It is, of course, equally important to see that there is no twist in the mainsail.

Some of the details for bending on the mainsail and jib of a Bermudan sloop areshown in the illustrations on pages 41–2, with the different types of equipment you may meet in practice. If the foot of the sail has to be laced to a spar, do it carefully and get the tension of the sail correct all along the spar. If the mainsail is made for a mast with a luff groove, it is sometimes necessary to wax the bolt rope.

Pay particular attention to any knots you make. Choose the correct one and make it correctly. You will find that in most cases where knots, bends and hitches have to be used, one knot is most suited to the particular job in hand and has probably been devised for it. To use the wrong knot, bend or hitch will only lead to trouble.

(10) If you are on moorings check the mooring rope is free, if at anchor
      check anchor is clear

When the sails are bent on, check that the mooring rope is free to be detached quickly and that the mooring buoy is on deck ready to be tossed overboard. Make your dinghy fast on to this if she is being left on the mooring.

(*a*) **Slip rope.** If your boat is made fast to the larger type of mooring buoy which is not taken aboard, a short pennant spliced into the bow is very useful as a SLIP ROPE. This can be passed through the eye of the buoy or, if the dinghy has been moored to the buoy, through the transom ring of the dinghy. The end is brought back on board and made fast until ready to sail.

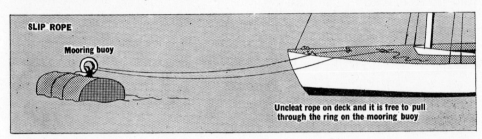

SLIP ROPE

Mooring buoy

Uncleat rope on deck and it is free to pull through the ring on the mooring buoy

If you are not on a mooring the boat will be lying at anchor. See that the anchor rope is clear to haul in. It may have become foul of the mooring warps or chains of near-by craft since it was last used. This often happens in a crowded anchorage. You will be in real trouble if you only discover a fouled anchor after y ur sails are hoisted and you are partly under way.

(*b*) **Starting anchor.** It is a good plan to heave short on the anchor warp before hoisting sail.

Make a practice of starting the anchor out of the ground and letting go again before you rig.

(11) Check buoyancy equipment of boat and personal buoyancy

See that BUOYANCY BAGS are inflated and securely fastened or that any other type of buoyancy is in good order. Check that your crew and yourself are wearing LIFE-JACKETS.

(12) Check crew is ready to get under way

When you have decided how you are going to get under way make sure your crew is ready before you give the order to cast off.

11. Learning to Sail: Stage Two-- Getting Under Way

Wind and tide

Tides ebb and flow each day round our coasts and winds blow and change direction. The wind will blow either in the same direction as the tide, against the tide or across the tide.

Both wind and tides influence the way in which boats lie at moorings or at anchor. Deep or fixed keel boats and boats which displace a great deal of water lie to the tide. They are said to be TIDE RODE. Some centre-board boats, and boats which displace little water and have a high free board or superstructure above the water-line generally lie to the wind. They are said to be WIND RODE. Some craft will lie across the tide under the influence of the wind. At slack water, most boats are on the move and no one can tell with certainty how they will lie eventually.

Where does the wind come from?

Before you hoist sail you must decide where the wind comes from in relation to the boat. If the boat is lying steadily in one direction, there are three answers to the question.

The wind may come from:

(i) For'ard of the beam of the boat

(ii) Aft of the beam of the boat

(iii) The wind is not clearly for'ard or clearly aft of the beam.

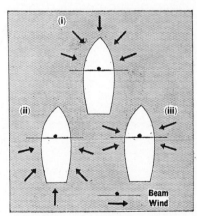

Wind for'ard of the beam

This is the case when wind and tide are in the same direction or when the boat is on tideless water. Should your boat lie to the wind rather than the tide, the wind will invariably be for'ard of the beam.

In this situation, the drill is clear:

95

(1) **Hoist the mainsail.** When the wind is for'ard of the beam, the boat will continue to lie quietly at the mooring even with the mainsail hoisted. The mainsail will flap, acting as a 'weathervane', and it will help to keep the boat head to wind.

Do not make the mainsheet fast because this may prevent the mainsail from flapping freely, it will fill with wind and you may start sailing.

(2) **Hoist the jib or foresail.** When the jib is hoisted the picture is quite different. In anything of a wind the jib will blow violently from side to side. This is known as a FLACKING JIB. It will twist round itself and tangle the jib sheets before you can do anything to stop it. Once the jib is hoisted lose no time in getting away, otherwise tie it to the forestay with tyers to prevent its wild behaviour.

(3) **Trim the sheets.** The boat will not move ahead while the sails are shaking in the wind. To TRIM THE SHEETS draw the jib sheet aft and haul in the mainsheet until the sails stop shaking. The sails are then drawing or full.

(4) **Weighing anchor or casting off mooring.** To WEIGH ANCHOR pull the boat forward on the anchor rope or chain or if the boat is a bigger one use the winch provided. If there is no winch and doing it by hand proves difficult sail the boat up gently over her anchor. When hauling on the chain or rope you will feel the anchor BREAK OUT and it may then be hauled aboard. If you are on a mooring cast off.

(5) **Sail away.** Once the boat is on the move continue to sail in the direction the boat has been pointing, i.e. sail against the wind or to windward. Alternatively, (a) PUT THE TILLER DOWN, turn into the wind, go about and sail to windward on the other tack, or (b) put the tiller up, BEAR AWAY and sail with the wind aft, i.e. run before the wind.

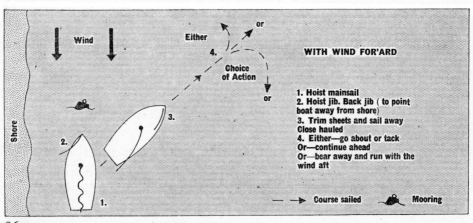

Wind

Either

Choice of Action

or

or

WITH WIND FOR'ARD

1. Hoist mainsail
2. Hoist jib. Back jib (to point boat away from shore)
3. Trim sheets and sail away Close hauled
4. Either—go about or tack Or—continue ahead Or—bear away and run with the wind aft

Shore

- - - ➤ Course sailed   Mooring

The helmsman sits to windward, i.e. on the side opposite to that on which the sail and boom are lying. To put the tiller down is to move it *away* from you, when you are sitting to windward. This will turn the boat's head up into the wind. The term HELM AWAY is sometimes used.

If you prefer, in a crowded anchorage, the jib or foresail need not be hoisted until the boat is clear. The boat will sail from the moorings under mainsail only.

Wind aft of the beam

This situation will arise only when wind and tide are in opposite directions and the weather tide is flowing so strongly as to overcome the force of the wind, causing boats which normally lie to the wind to lie to the tide. The WEATHER TIDE is the weather-going tide, i.e. it flows against the wind. The expression WIND AGAINST TIDE is more commonly used.

This case will also arise on a tideless river when the flow of water is against the prevailing wind.

Your course of action is clear and definite:

(1) **Get the mainsail ready** for a quick hoist, but do not hoist.

(2) **Hoist the jib first.**

(3) **Cast off the mooring, trim the jib sheet. With the wind aft you will get under way without mainsail and with jib alone.**

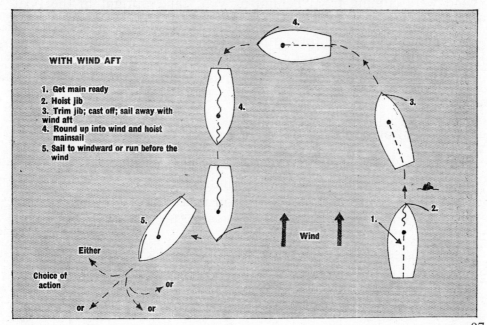

WITH WIND AFT

1. Get main ready
2. Hoist jib
3. Trim jib; cast off; sail away with wind aft
4. Round up into wind and hoist mainsail
5. Sail to windward or run before the wind

(4) **Round up into the wind and hoist the mainsail.** When you are in clear water with room to manoeuvre, put the tiller down, round up into the wind and hoist the mainsail.

(5) **Sail to windward or run before the wind.**

Why not hoist the mainsail first? It is practically impossible to do so. With the wind aft, as soon as the head of the sail starts to go up it will be pressed forward by the wind and it will get caught under the shrouds or crosstrees. Even if you overcome this difficulty the top batten in the sail will also get caught. As the sail fills and is pressed forward it is turned at right angles to the slot of the luff groove and the luff rope sticks in the groove. The same thing happens in the case of track and track hanks. The sail is stiff and sometimes impossible to hoist. Worse, as soon as the mainsail is partly up the boat sails forward. She is soon at the end of the scope of the mooring rope or chain and will turn wildly. There is confusion of the first order.

Wind dead on the beam or doubtful

When the wind is coming from just aft of the beam, is dead on the beam, or is just for'ard of the beam, you may wonder what action to take. There are two courses:

(1) **Treat the situation as if the wind is aft of the beam,** i.e. as if the wind were coming from behind as you stand upright in the boat facing the bows.

Prepare the mainsail for a quick hoist; hoist the jib first, and trim. Cast off the mooring and sail away running before the wind.

With way on and room to manoeuvre round up into the wind, i.e. put the tiller down and turn the boat head to wind into a position where the sails will shake. Hoist the mainsail. This is a perfectly safe and straightforward decision to have made.

(2) **Sheer the boat up into the wind on her moorings,** i.e. coax the boat to lie fully and clearly to the wind.

See that the centre-board and drop rudder are fully up. Do not lower them until you are ready to sail away. This reduces the influences of the tide.

Partly hoist the mainsail and as it fills in the wind the boat will gather way. Put the tiller down to bring the boat up into the wind and stop her moving forward. You will still be on your mooring. No attempt should yet have been made to cast off.

98

The boat may by now be lying to the wind. If so, hoist the mainsail quickly, cast off and sail away.

(3) **If in doubt go back to course** (1).

If there is little room to manoeuvre with a rough sea or a very strong tide running, the second method is not recommended as it will probably prove unsuccessful. In any case of doubt, or at the first sign of failure or difficulty, go back to the first alternative, i.e. treat the situation as if the wind is aft of the beam.

Special problems in getting under way

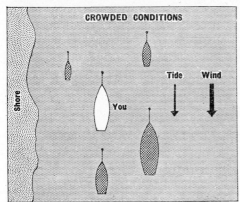

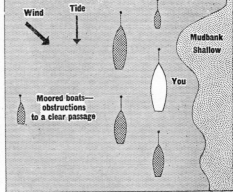

In crowded conditions

(1) **The sternboard.** Sometimes an anchorage or harbour is very crowded and there is not much room to manoeuvre. This makes getting under way more difficult.

One way out of the difficulty is to use a STERNBOARD. In making a sternboard a boat moves astern, i.e. backwards stern first. The rudder and tiller action is opposite to normal. To move the bows to starboard put the tiller to starboard. To move the bows to port put the tiller to port. When making a sternboard the turning action of a boat is much slower than when going ahead. More often the boat is moved astern under the action of tide alone but sometimes it is a combination of both wind and tide.

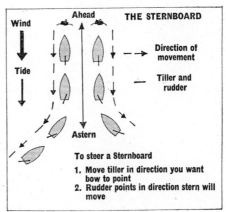

AN UNINTENTIONAL STERNBOARD. A sternboard can be made with sails down. It can also be made with the sails hoisted, that is, set, trimmed and drawing properly. If this happens it is because the tide is more powerful than the wind, and although the sails are full the boat will not move forward in the direction you are pointing. Once this happens there is little you can do to avoid this kind of sternboard which is to your disadvantage and is not intended.

DELIBERATE STERNBOARDS. The sternboard used to get clear away from a crowded situation is different in that it is deliberate.

How to make a deliberate stern-board. The wind is forward of the beam and the full sail set. With room to move, the boat would sail to windward away from her mooring, but there is an obstacle in the way. Make a sternboard in order to sail the boat through the gap to reach clear water. To do this you need not trim the sails fully. Let the *tide* carry the boat astern.

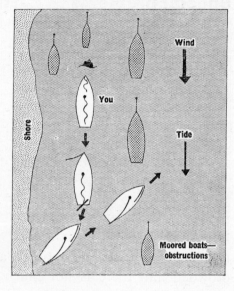

Moored boats—
obstructions

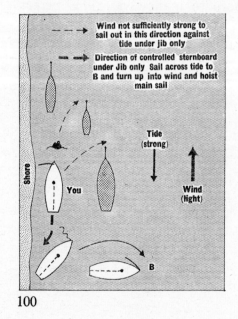

Wind not sufficiently strong to sail out in this direction against tide under jib only

Direction of controlled sternboard under jib only. Sail across tide to B and turn up into wind and hoist main sail

Tide (strong)

Wind (light)

You

B

Shore

How to get under way with the wind aft using the jib only. The tide is running strongly and the jib alone does not provide enough sail area to move the boat *ahead* against the tide. The immediate object is to move the boat to clear water with room to manoeuvre. This is done by making a controlled sternboard. Once there turn head to wind and hoist the mainsail.

(2) **Kedging out.** If you are hemmed in by other boats on your mooring and find you can not sail out safely, you could try KEDGING.

If you look round, you will probably see a patch of water quite close to you where you could get under way if only you were there and not on your buoy.

Put your anchor in the dinghy. Coil the warp down on top of it, make the other end fast on board, pull the dinghy away to a point a little up-tide from the good spot, paying out the warp as you go. When you get there, heave the anchor over and pull back to your boat. Make your dinghy fast. Haul in the slack of the warp, cast off the mooring buoy and heave out to your anchor.

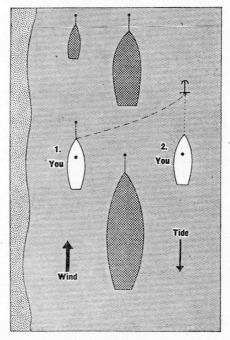

This trick of course is only used in large craft as small ones can be moved out or towed out to a suitable place and anchored there before rigging up.

Getting under way in a una rig or catboat with the wind aft

If your boat has a Bermudan mainsail only, how do you get under way with the wind aft? There is no jib under which to sail out into clear water where you can bring the boat head to wind and set the mainsail. The best way to solve the problem is to move your mooring or anchor rope aft and let the boat lie stern first. In this position the mainsail can be set head to wind. If your boat is a lugsail catboat the sail will usually go up just as easily with the wind aft. It is much easier to hoist with the wind aft than other types of mainsail.

Launching from a shore

If you keep your boat ashore in a dinghy park or trail her by car to the coast or inland water, she can be launched quite successfully from a causeway or jetty running down to water-level or from a beach or hard.

While your boat is still ashore get her ready for sailing as if she

101

were on a mooring or at anchor. Bend on the sails before you are afloat.

Take the boat to the water's edge on a launching trolley. The boat is often launched stern first.

Then decide in what order to hoist your sails, and how to sail away.

Your decision will depend on the strength of the wind and its direction in relation to the shore. There are three sets of conditions:

(1) The wind may be blowing on the shore. If this is the case you are on a lee shore.

(2) The wind may be blowing off the shore. In this case you will be on a weather shore.

(3) It may be blowing along the shore.

The diagrams show you what to do in different conditions.

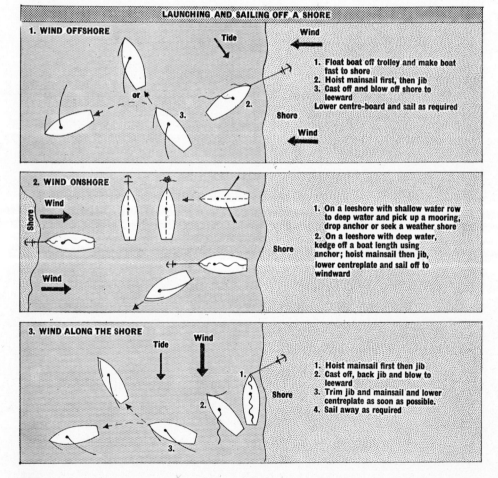

LAUNCHING AND SAILING OFF A SHORE

1. WIND OFFSHORE
Tide
Wind
1. Float boat off trolley and make boat fast to shore
2. Hoist mainsail first, then jib
3. Cast off and blow off shore to leeward
Lower centre-board and sail as required
Shore
Wind

2. WIND ONSHORE
Wind
Shore
Wind
1. On a leeshore with shallow water row to deep water and pick up a mooring, drop anchor or seek a weather shore
2. On a leeshore with deep water, kedge off a boat length using anchor; hoist mainsail then jib, lower centreplate and sail off to windward
Shore

3. WIND ALONG THE SHORE
Tide
Wind
Shore
1. Hoist mainsail first then jib
2. Cast off, back jib and blow to leeward
3. Trim jib and mainsail and lower centreplate as soon as possible.
4. Sail away as required

12. Learning to Sail: Stage Three—Sailing

Helmsman and crew

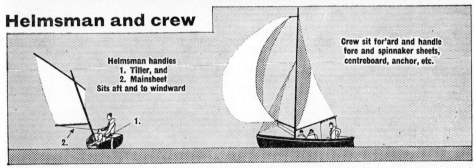

Helmsman handles
1. Tiller, and
2. Mainsheet
Sits aft and to windward

Crew sit for'ard and handle
fore and spinnaker sheets,
centreboard, anchor, etc.

The **helmsman** steers the boat and in a dinghy holds the mainsheet as well as the tiller. He stays aft and usually sits to windward. The helmsman is in charge. He gives orders and receives reports from the crew.

The **crew,** of which there may be one or more people, handle the foresheets and spinnaker, adjust the centre-board and they are responsible for the anchor or moorings. In small boats the crew stay for'ard and sit either to windward or leeward to trim the boat. The crew reports back to the helmsman.

A **watch** is made up of the helmsman and crew. If a boat is cruising or racing continuously day and night several watches may be needed.

Two or more watches will make up the SHIP'S COMPLEMENT or SHIP'S COMPANY.

Sailing to windward

This is also known as BEATING, SAILING CLOSE-HAULED or ON THE WIND and involves *sailing as close as you can into a head wind.*

Position of helmsman and crew:

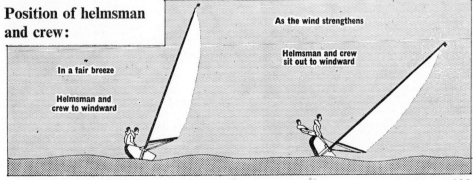

In a fair breeze

Helmsman and crew to windward

As the wind strengthens

Helmsman and crew sit out to windward

(1) **Sailing the boat upright.** In a fair breeze, the helmsman and crew sit to windward. As the wind rises it is important to get as much weight as possible to windward to correct the heel of the boat to leeward. The crew has to SIT OUT, i.e. to sit up on the gunwale or side-deck. If the wind rises still more and the heel to leeward increases, the crew has to correct this by getting as much weight as possible outside the boat. The helmsman may also have to sit out.

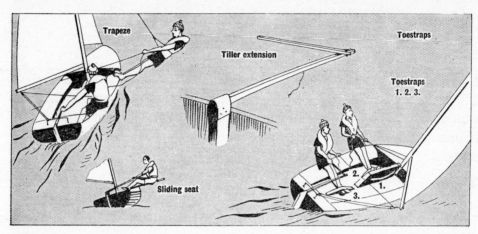

There are various devices which help them to do this without over-balancing: TOE-STRAPS or a TRAPEZE to help the crew and a TILLER EXTENSION to allow the helmsman to sit out. Sitting out is carried to the extreme in Hornet class racing dinghies which have a sliding seat for the crew right outside the boat.

In light airs the crew and/or sometimes the helmsman sit to leeward to trim the boat to leeward.

(2) **Trimming the boat fore and aft.** Small boats usually sail better to windward if the helmsman and crew sit further for'ard so that the fore-foot is in the water. The position of lateral resistance which depends on how the hull is immersed is then improved and drag aft at the transom is reduced.

104

Position of the centre-board

When sailing to windward the centre-board should be *fully down*. It may be adjusted to give the right amount of weather helm according to the strength of the wind.

Handling the tiller

The helmsman steers the boat with the tiller and *if he always sits to windward* it helps him to learn to move the tiller instinctively.

Put tiller away or down

Wind

Boat sails up into wind or luffs.

Push the TILLER DOWN, i.e. TILLER AWAY FROM YOU and the boat luffs up to WINDWARD, i.e. up into the wind until the sails flutter and are a-shake.

Put tiller towards you or up

Boat bears away and wind frees.

Move the TILLER UP, i.e. TILLER TOWARDS YOU and the boat BEARS AWAY and gives the sails more apparent wind. If you continue to bear away EASE the sheets that control the sails.

In a well-designed boat only a small movement of the tiller and rudder is necessary. Excess movement causes the rudder to act as a brake.

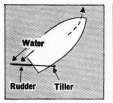

Water

Rudder   Tiller

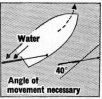

Water

40°

Angle of movement necessary

Trim of the sails

Sails are trimmed by adjusting the sheets which control them. When sailing close-hauled the aft end of the boom of the mainsail will lie over the boat's quarter. The sails will need little adjustment except to meet changes in wind direction and to spill the wind in gusts.

Sailing close-hauled the sails should be ASLEEP so that the boat is sailing FULL AND BY, i.e. with the sails just full of wind so that they do not tremble.

If you sail too close to the wind and PINCH HER the sails will begin to flutter at the luff and to lose wind.

To keep her sailing full and by, the way in which the boat is pointing has to be altered to meet changes in the wind direction. To bring the boat closer to the wind LUFF by putting the tiller down, i.e. away from you if you are sitting to windward. To bring the boat off the wind to give the sails more apparent wind, BEAR AWAY by moving the tiller up towards you.

On a beat it is necessary to luff and bear away alternately to meet subtle wind changes. To help you do this keep one eye on the burgee or racing flag and the other on the luff of the mainsail or jib. Before starting out make sure that the luff of both mainsail and jib are set up as taut as possible. If the luff of either sail backs towards you, the boat is sailing too close to the wind. Bear away a little so that the sail fills. If there is a tremble or flutter at the leech and this is not due to the sail being distorted or mis-shapen, then the same applies. The most likely combination is for the luff of the jib to back slightly and the leech of the mainsail to tremble. If the sails are asleep and you are sailing full and by keep a continuous check on the way you are pointing to windward by luffing very gently, just enough to make the luff of the jib back slightly and prove that you are pointing correctly.

Spilling the wind

In a puff or gust of wind the boat may heel dangerously to the point of capsizing unless you SPILL THE WIND. There are two ways of spilling the wind.

(1) **Luffing up.** In a moderate gust spill the wind by sailing closer to it. Put you tiller down or away from you to bring the boat's head into the wind until the sails shake and lose wind. This is LUFFING UP. Keep the boat moving with the sails just a-shake until the puff is over. Avoid luffing too much into the headwind otherwise you will lose way completely and the boat will be in irons.

(2) **Easing the sheets.** In broken water do not luff up but EASE THE SHEETS. Avoid letting the boat stop or slow down too much. Keep her moving and sail through the danger period with the sails just a-shake. Haul the sheets in again when the gust is over and you are out of danger from heeling too much to leeward.

In a dinghy never make the sheets fast and avoid standing up in the boat.

106

Coming about

At the end of a windward tack or board you have to COME ABOUT. Warn the crew with the order READY ABOUT. Push the tiller away from you *gently*. If you do this too suddenly the rudder will act as a brake and the boat will have difficulty in coming round. As you put the tiller down call 'LEE-OH' to the crew. 'LEE-OH' means 'I am now going to go about,' i.e. 'Your weather side is about to become the lee side.' On the command 'Lee-oh' the crew releases the foresheet —not before. The boat turns up into the wind. If the tiller action is correct and the crew has released the foresheet, the head of the boat will pass through the wind and the boom and mainsail will cross from one side of the boat to the other. The helmsman and crew also cross over and take up their positions on the new windward side. In a strong breeze both helmsman and crew have to sit out as quickly as possible to counterbalance the heel to leeward on the new tack. The helmsman sheets in the mainsail to the correct position so that the boat is now sailing full and by on her new board or tack. The crew sheets in the foresail correspondingly. It is sometimes necessary to sheet the foresail just after you go through the eye of the wind before the mainsail is full because it requires great strength to sheet it in if there is already some wind in the sail. But this needs to be done with care and eased off if necessary when the mainsail is set.

As the boat's head passes through the wind she is said to be IN STAYS. If due to an error of judgment it is difficult to get out of the position she is said to be IN IRONS. Usually the boat's head will PAY OFF in one direction or the other by BACKING THE JIB or HOLDING THE JIB TO WEATHER.

A boat gets into irons by faulty timing in jib handling. The jib must not be sheeted in on the new side until after the boat's head has passed through the eye of the wind or the head will be forced back from whence it has come; the boat will go into irons or even go back on the old tack. If a boat's head is sluggish in coming round after the jib has been released and let fly, re-sheet the jib on the old side for a few seconds. This is known as holding the jib to weather or backing the jib. The pressure of the wind on the jib will force the boat's head to come round. If the jib is held aback too long the boat falls away to leeward and slows down.

If you have a wooden centre-board that floats up, see that it is still down after coming about.

107

Warn the crew when you decide to come about with the call 'READY ABOUT' and then order; 'LEE-OH' when you actually put the tiller down.

Reaching

Getting to this point of sailing from being close-hauled
Pull the tiller towards you and ease the sheets. Warn the crew what you are doing by saying 'BEARING AWAY'. The boat's head will bear away, the wind will free and come more abeam.

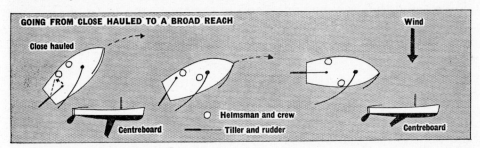

As soon as you cease to be close-hauled you are on a fine reach. If you bear away still further the wind will come abeam. If you continue to bear away the wind will draw aft to the beam and you are on a broad reach.

Getting to this point of sailing from running before the wind with the wind aft or nearly aft
Push the tiller gently away from you and haul in the sheets. The wind will draw forward and you are again on a broad reach. If you turn further up into the wind you go on to a fine reach.

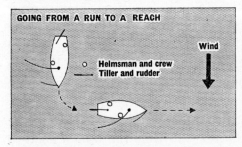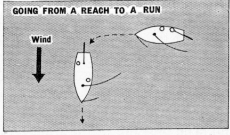

Reaching is the easiest position of sailing. The wind is free and you can choose the direction in which you wish to sail. The boat sits more upright and is not pressed so hard. It is also the fastest position of sailing and light boats of the right shape are likely to plane.

Trim of the sails

The boom and sails lie out at an angle of about 45 degrees to the fore-and-aft line of the boat. With the wind free you can sail up and down a river or through a channel as you wish. It is always wise to keep to the windward side and avoid the lee shore. When you are reaching it is necessary to trim the sails all the time to test the set of the sails and also adjust them to the wind and course. *Release and pay out the sheets until the sails begin to shake.* As soon as the sails shake, haul in the sheets until the sails are just asleep. Only a small movement of the sheets is necessary. The correct order for slackening away the sheets slightly is CHECK FORESHEET or CHECK MAINSHEET and for hauling them in AFT FORESHEET or AFT MAINSHEET.

Position of helmsman and crew

The helmsman sits to windward but because of the reduced tendency to heel the crew often sits to leeward in a light breeze. In a stronger wind both helmsman and crew will sit to windward and sometimes move aft to help the boat to lift forward and start planing.

Position of centre-board

The centre-board should be between half and three-quarters of the way down. Check your leeway by looking aft at the wake and lower the centre-plate if the wake shows much leeway. The helm balance is also a good guide to the position of the centre-board when reaching. In strong winds a good deal of weather helm develops. This can often be remedied by raising the centre-board.

Running with the wind aft

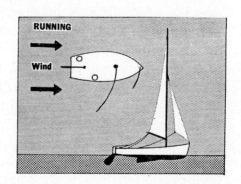

To change your point of sailing from a broad reach to running with the wind aft pull the TILLER TO-WARDS YOU, FREE THE SHEETS and BEAR AWAY. The wind will draw aft over the boat's quarter. The boom is roughly at right angles to the fore-and-aft line of the boat.

Position of helmsman and crew

Helmsman and crew sit aft. The boat should be kept upright or trimmed slightly to leeward, i.e. the same side as the boom. Helmsman sits to windward, crew to leeward.

109

Position of the centre-board

The pressure of the wind comes from aft and the boat is blown along like a leaf. Lateral resistance created by the pressure of the water on the hull and centre-plate is no longer needed to help the boat sail and the centre-plate can be brought right up.

If the boat rolls, lower the centre-plate a little. If this does not solve the problem and the boat develops a dangerous roll it may be necessary to give up running with the wind dead aft and to sail on a broad reach.

Two dangers when running

When running the wind appears to be much less and all seems quiet and peaceful. This sense of security is false because two dangers are always present. They can easily be avoided by correct action but they are serious in heavy weather and broken water.

(1) **A standing accidental gybe.** The ACCIDENTAL GYBE is what happens when the boom and mainsail crash from one side of the boat to the other. When sailing with the wind dead aft or nearly aft with a

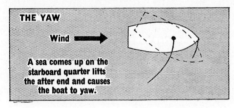

following sea the boat tends to YAW. To YAW is to move slightly off course, first on one side and then the other and the direction of the wind over the boat's quarter varies accordingly. When sailing with the wind aft the helmsman must be on the look-out for the signs that a gybe is imminent. When the jib or headsail wants to set on the opposite side of the boat from the mainsail you are sailing GOOSE-WINGED. This shows that the wind has drawn across. If you continue on this point of sailing you will be sailing BY THE LEE and the danger is that the mainsail may follow the headsail over with a crash. Before this happens the boom begins to lift or cock and

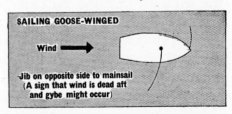

the wind plays on the back of the mainsail. The burgee will soon show the wind to be on the wrong side. The wise course of action, particularly in broken water, is to push the tiller slightly away from you and sail with the wind more over the boat's quarter.

110

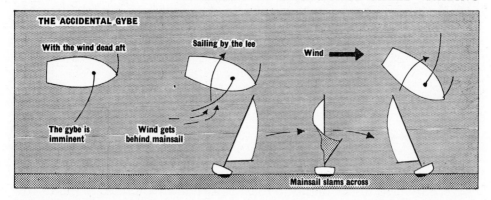

(2) **Broaching to.** When a boat BROACHES TO, she takes charge and turns—half slides—sharply into the wind. This is sudden and she comes beam on to the wind and seas with boom right out. The boat is nearly stopped and the boom may dip into the water. She heels hard and quickly and in a dinghy it is almost impossible to avoid a capsize. The solution is to be very watchful and to correct early with the tiller and rudder any tendency to turn in this way.

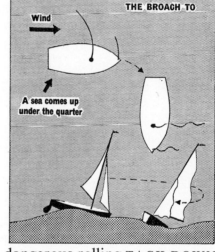

How to avoid the dangers: tack down wind. To avoid the accidental gybe and the broach to and to reduce dangerous rolling TACK DOWN WIND. Sail in your general direction on a broad reach. This will take

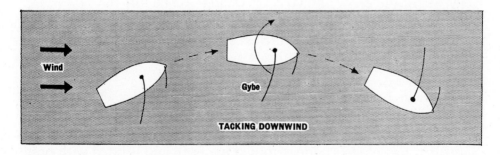

you slightly off course but you will avoid having the wind dead aft. To get more or less back on course turn, after a time, and sail back to your objective by a broad reach on the opposite tack. To turn the boat either put her into the wind, sailing a full circle, or make a deliberate gybe.

Sail under headsail alone
Used for:
(1) Getting away from and back to moorings when the wind is aft of the beam.
(2) For ordinary sailing when gear connected with using the mainsail is damaged or the mainsail itself is torn and you have to make your return under headsail only.
(3) For running before the wind in bad weather and when it is imprudent any longer to go to windward.

Only the very best designed and balanced centre-board and keel boats will beat to windward under headsail only and even then their progress is slow and they sail much less close to the wind.

Generally, reaching and running before the wind is quite easy under headsail only. The sail need only be sheeted and trimmed on the correct side of the boat to suit your sailing. A great advantage in heavy weather and broken seas is that with the wind dead aft the danger of an accidental gybe is removed.

Make a deliberate gybe
A DELIBERATE GYBE, that is, a turn with the wind aft, is not so dangerous, but even a deliberate gybe is to be avoided in heavy weather. A deliberate gybe is controlled and the helmsman is not caught unaware.

To make a deliberate gybe:
(1) Warn the crew. 'READY TO GYBE—GYBE OH'
(2) Haul in the mainsheet and with it the boom and sail.
(3) Turn the boat's head further off the wind by pulling the tiller towards you. The wind will draw dead aft then change to the new side.
(4) As the boom and mainsail move to the new lee side the helmsman and crew move to trim the boat on the new windward side.
(5) Under careful control, let out the mainsheet, boom and sail.
(6) If your boat has a loose-footed mainsail and is fitted with brails, then brail up before you gybe and re-set the mainsail when on the new tack.

112

Picking up moorings or anchoring

THREE SIMPLE RULES IN TIDAL WATERS

(1) Always sail on to your moorings or anchorage against the tide
Check this by looking at the position of other boats on their moorings. They will be lying into the tide. Approach your moorings in the fore-and-aft line of other boats.

(2) With the wind aft, approach under headsail only
If, in order to obey this rule, you arrive at your mooring or anchorage with the wind aft, approach it under headsail only, having turned up into the wind and taken down the mainsail well in advance.

(3) Wind for'ard of the beam
If you obey rule (1) and arrive at your mooring or anchorage with the wind forward of the beam, take way off the boat by slacking the foresheets right off and by easing the mainsheet; (*a*) make fast your mooring or drop your anchor, (*b*) lower the headsails first, (*c*) lower the mainsail afterwards.

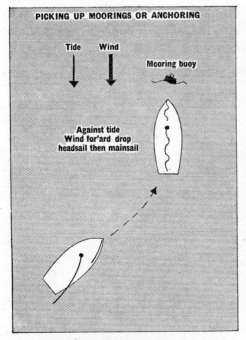 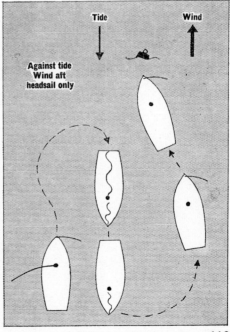

TWO SIMPLE RULES FOR COMING INTO A SHORE OR RIVER BANK

Wind on-shore, headsail only
(1) If the wind is blowing on-shore steer for the shore under headsail only having turned up into the wind and taken down the mainsail well in advance of reaching the shore or bank. In very light airs it may be necessary to keep the mainsail set. Order your crew to jump ashore immediately the boat touches.

Wind off-shore, full sail
(2) If the wind is blowing off-shore steer for the shore under full sail.
    (*a*) Turn up into the wind.
    (*b*) Lower headsail.
    (*c*) Make fast to the shore or bank.
    (*d*) Lower mainsail.

Stowing ship
(1) Have a set place for everything to be left aboard and stow all your gear carefully. Coil and make fast all cordage. Leave your boat clean and dry inside.

(2) Examine all equipment to see if anything needs attention. This is the best time to plan and even to do some of the day-to-day care and maintenance.

(3) Unless the sails remain fixed to spars, unbend all sails and take them ashore. If they are encrusted with salt or wet with salt water rinse and dry them carefully before stowing away in the sail-bag.

(4) Check and double-check that your boat is secure on her mooring.

The wind and the sails

Aerodynamics

(1) The cross-section of a sail is a curved line and the sail is a curved sheet. This shape is known as an AEROFOIL.

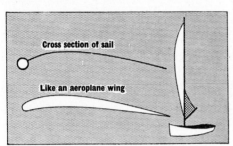

Cross section of sail

Like an aeroplane wing

(2) Air flows fastest on the longest side of a curved line. This is characteristic of an aerofoil. If the air flows aft on both sides of a sail, the path of the air on the lee side is longer and the air on the lee side flows faster.

(3) A flow of air moving fast along a surface reduces the air pressure acting on that surface.

To demonstrate this, blow along the convex surface of a slightly curved sheet of paper. The paper will be sucked towards the side of the fast-moving stream of air.

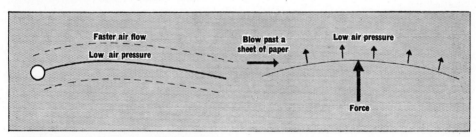

Faster air flow

Low air pressure

Blow past a sheet of paper

Low air pressure

Force

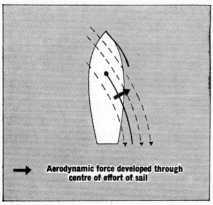

Aerodynamic force developed through centre of effort of sail

(4) The stream of air which moves faster on the lee side of the sail reduces the air pressure on that side of the sail. A force is developed at right angles to the sail on the lee side. This force moves in the leeward direction, and acts through the centre of effort of the sail.

115

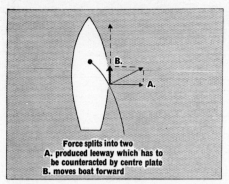

Force splits into two
A. produced leeway which has to
be counteracted by centre plate
B. moves boat forward

(5) The force can be thought of as split into two parts:

(*a*) The part which moves the boat sideways and is resisted by the water acting on the keel, and

(*b*) The part which moves the boat in the forward direction. The boat shape helps this.

(6) When sailing close-hauled the faster the flow of air past the sail the greater the force developed at right angles to the sail on the lee side and the faster the boat moves forward.

(7) As the wind frees, the direct pressure on the weather side of the sail becomes more and more important until, with the wind aft, it outweighs the effect of 'suction' on the lee side.

Comparison with aircraft wings

The sails of a boat work rather like the wings of an aeroplane but some features are different. The comparable features are shown below:

Similarities

THE SAIL: THE AEROPLANE WING

(1) Both are aerofoils.

(2) In both, the most effective part is just aft of the leading edge or luff.

(3) The least useful part is the tip of the wing or the peak of the sail.

(4) Headsails in a boat act like the second wing of a biplane and smooth out eddies in the flow of air behind the mainsail. A headsail sheeted in too close backwinds the mainsail and disturbs the smooth flow of air. This is known as 'biplane interference' in aircraft.

Differences

THE SAIL	THE AEROPLANE WING
(1) Is porous and lets air escape through it.	(1) Is non-porous and makes full use of the air-flow.
(2) Is soft and flexible, twists and loses its designed shape.	(2) Is rigid and retains its shape better than the sail.
(3) Is mounted vertically and gives a forward movement.	(3) Is mounted horizontally and gives an upward movement or lift.
(4) The sailing boat moves slowly—often more slowly than the wind. Therefore her sails are working against an apparent headwind only part of the time. Often the wind is aft of the sails.	(4) The aeroplane moves very fast—much faster than the wind—thus its wings are always working against a strong apparent headwind.

Getting a better airflow

Smoothness of the sailcloth

Rough fibres in the sailcloth interfere with the smooth flow of air past the mainsail, that is why cotton sails are better than flax and, in turn, Nylon and 'Terylene' are better than cotton.

Synthetic fibres are also more efficient because they are less porous.

Streamlined masts

The mast disturbs the airflow by setting up eddies along the sail. To get over this difficulty some designers streamline the mast by making it pear-shaped instead of round, but this is not the complete answer because the sail is set at varying angles to the mast. The process has to be carried a stage further by making the mast rotate so that streamlining can be effective at whatever angle the sail is set.

Weight of the mast

A tall heavy mast increases the tendency of the boat to heel and this reduces efficiency in sailing to windward.

To reduce the weight, masts are made of light timber, e.g. spruce. They are usually hollow and laminated to keep them strong and rigid as well as light.

Rigging

The rigging which supports the mast also hinders the flow of air. To get over this problem designers now try to reduce the number of stays and thickness of wire, to use smooth rod rigging in place of wire rope and to put the halyards inside the hollow mast.

Several racing dinghies today have unstayed ROTATING MASTS.

Boat features which affect sailing

Heeling

The efficiency of sailing is affected by too much heel, twists in the sails and the action of the centre-board or keel.

Sail your boat as near upright as possible. The ideal position is for a boat to have a slight *heel to leeward*. It looks wrong and it is *incorrect* ever to sail your boat with a *heel to windward*.

117

Too much heel to leeward is dangerous and inefficient
The boat will not sail as fast because:

(1) The effective sail area and the effective area of the centre-board or keel are both reduced. She has less driving power and less resistance to leeway so that she is unable to hold up to windward and falls away from the wind.

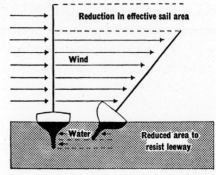

(2) Heeling also causes the wind to take an upward diagonal path across the sail which presses the sail downwards instead of forwards. The boat turns up violently into the wind. This action is known as GRIPING. It has to be corrected by holding the tiller up to windward. The rudder acts as a brake and this slows down the boat even more.

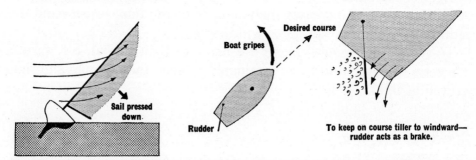

(3) The lee gunwale gets too near the water and, in a broken sea, water is bound to come inboard. The water will add weight in the wrong place and make the boat heel still further. This may lead to a capsize.

(4) The designed water-line shape is distorted and becomes less efficient.

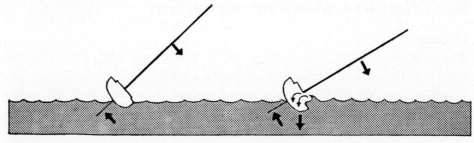

Shapes of waterline

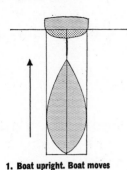
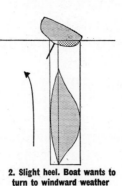
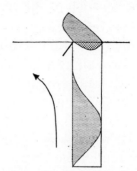

1. Boat upright. Boat moves straight ahead

2. Slight heel. Boat wants to turn to windward weather helm to check

3. Great heel. Boat strains to windward and 'gripes' great weather helm needed.

How to avoid too much heeling

(*a*) Reef the sails in a strong breeze.

(*b*) Ease the sheet and let the sails shake in strong puffs of wind.

(*c*) Sit out the boat early.

The boat will sail faster in heavy weather if these steps are taken to avoid heeling.

Twist in sails

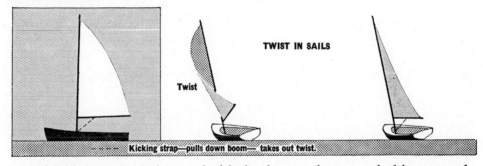

TWIST IN SAILS

Twist

Kicking strap—pulls down boom— takes out twist.

A kicking strap helps to hold the boom down and this not only increases the efficiency of the sails but reduces the risk of an accidental gybe when running with the wind aft. The disadvantage of a kicking strap is that in a small boat it gets in the way of the crew.

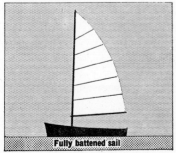

Fully battened sail

In the Far East sailing craft often had their sails fully battened and this overcomes the disadvantages of twist. Shape is thus improved in use and the flow preserved without flattening. Many classes of racing boats now permit fully battened sails and this adds to their efficiency and speed.

119

The function of the centre-board or keel

To prevent leeway. A boat makes more leeway when sailing to windward than when sailing with the wind free. She makes hardly any leeway sailing with the wind aft.

The centre-board, dagger plate or keel helps to prevent leeway because it is deep and functions in 'solid water' which is undisturbed by the movement of the hull near the surface.

To work well a centre-board should be streamlined so that it does not hinder the forward movement of the boat. It must be strong and is usually made of wood up to 1 inch thick or sheet-metal up to $\frac{5}{16}$ inch thick. It should be as deep as possible in relation to the size of the boat—3 to 5 feet for a boat 14 to 18 feet long. The width should be about a third of the depth.

To provide ballast. The modern centre-board is light and is not intended to do more than resist leeway, but the fixed keel supplies outside ballast to the hull. Ballast or weight placed as low as possible helps a boat to remain upright and stable.

The work of the centre-board when under way

(1) The centre-board is less effective when the boat reduces speed. If the wind drops when you are sailing to windward and slows the boat, bear away so that the boat points less high into the wind and sails more free. (2) The centre-board is also less effective in choppy water. When the sea is very broken sail less close to the wind and more free. (3) The amount of leeway varies from the maximum when sailing close-hauled to the minimum when running with the wind aft. The centre-board is adjusted according to the point of sailing. It should be:

Right down when close-hauled.	Half down when reaching.	Right up when running.

A little centre-plate is sometimes lowered to counteract the roll when running. (4) Adjusting the centre-board may also help to preserve helm balance.

Helm balance

Sail plan and underwater surface of hull give helm balance
(1) **Sail plan.** The wind energy absorbed by the sails acts through a point known as the CENTRE OF EFFORT of the sail plan. It is found geometrically as shown.

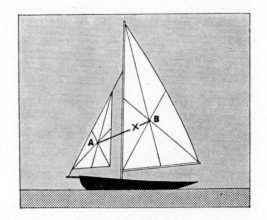

1. Bisect angles of each triangle and get centre of areas of foresail and mainsail.

2. Calculate area of foresail and mainsail and get proportion of one to the other, e.g. 1:3.

3. Join the two points A and B and divide this line in this proportion with the smaller part away from the smaller sail. Mark the point X. X is the Centre of Effort of the Sail plan.

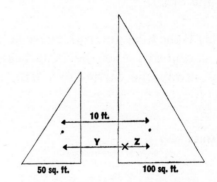

With a Gaff Mainsail it has first to be divided into two triangles to determine its centre. C and D are the centres of each triangle and A the centre of the gaff mainsail.

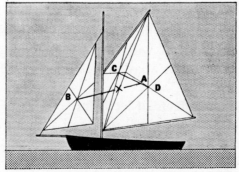

121

(2) **Underwater surface.** The sideways slip of the hull is resisted by its underwater surface mainly through the action of the keel or centre-board. This underwater surface also has a CENTRE OF LATERAL RESISTANCE.

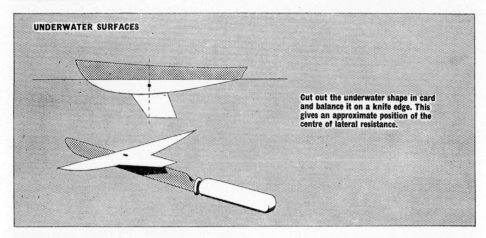

UNDERWATER SURFACES

Cut out the underwater shape in card and balance it on a knife edge. This gives an approximate position of the centre of lateral resistance.

(3) **Putting the two together.** When the boat is under way the two centres act together to form a COUPLE. The boat may pivot one way or the other.

(*a*) If the tiller and rudder are held centrally and the boat bears away she carries LEE HELM.

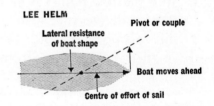

LEE HELM

Pivot or couple

Lateral resistance of boat shape

Boat moves ahead

Centre of effort of sail

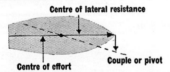

WEATHER HELM

Centre of lateral resistance

Centre of effort

Couple or pivot

(*b*) If the tiller and rudder are held centrally and the boat turns up into the wind she carries WEATHER HELM.

(*c*) If the tiller and rudder are held central and the boat sails straight ahead with the tiller pulling gently away from you she has slight weather helm and is well balanced.

Three effects of lee helm

(1) The boat will only sail straight ahead if the tiller is held down to leeward.

(2) The boat's head always tends to bear away.

(3) The tiller pushes towards you and great physical force is often required to hold the tiller away from you or even central.

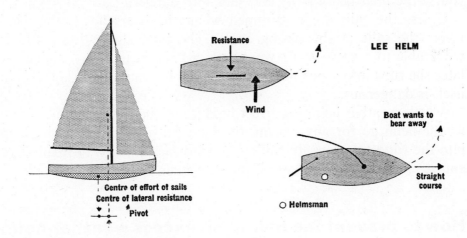

Two effects of weather helm

(1) The boat will only sail straight ahead if the tiller is held up to windward.
(2) The boat's head struggles to turn up to windward.

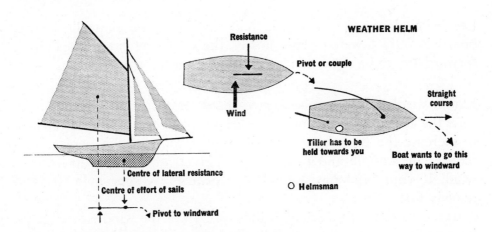

Lack of helm balance—its disadvantages

(1) Excess lee and weather helm are uncomfortable.
(2) If the tiller and rudder are held off centre to correct either lee helm or weather helm, the rudder acts as a brake. There is loss of power and wasted wind energy.
(3) Lee helm may make a boat very difficult to tack or come about.

123

Lee helm is dangerous at all times

When the tiller is released or the helmsman fails to sail a straight course the boat bears away and sails into danger.

Unless the sails are re-trimmed when she bears away, the wind meets the sails at the wrong angle. The boat slows down and is vulnerable to a KNOCK-DOWN PUFF. As she bears away, sooner or later she runs into a position where a gybe becomes likely and this in itself is dangerous.

A little weather helm is correct because of the safety factor. If you let the helm go for any reason, the boat sails gently and quietly up into the wind to safety. In sailing to windward it helps to maintain a course close to the wind even if the helmsman fails to concentrate.

How to prevent lee helm and excess weather helm

Lift or lower the centre-board

If you lift or lower the centre-board when under way this will alter the position of the centre of lateral resistance and improve helm balance.

Lee helm—lower centre-board. With lee helm see that the centre-board is fully lowered. This moves the centre of lateral resistance forward and reduces the tendency of the boat to bear away.

Excess weather helm—raise centre-board. With excess weather helm raise the centre-board to bring the centre of lateral resistance aft and to increase the proportion of sail plan forward of this centre. This reduces the couple and prevents the boat from turning up into the wind. If your boat has a tendency towards weather helm try this remedy first.

HELM BALANCE varies with the strength of the wind, speed of the boat and point of sailing, so that CENTRE-BOARD adjustment is very important to get the best out of your boat.

Shift ballast

Trim the boat a little more by the head either by sitting further for'ard or shifting ballast to correct lee helm. Trim by the stern to correct weather helm.

Alter position of mast

This enables you to move the whole sail plan fore or aft and to alter the centre of effort of the sails. To counteract lee helm rake the mast aft and to counteract excess weather helm rake the mast forward. If raking is not sufficient the mast position may have to be moved.

Alter relative size of mainsail and headsails

With lee helm use a bigger mainsail and/or a smaller headsail, and with weather helm use a smaller mainsail and/or a bigger headsail.

Lee helm sometimes occurs when a mainsail is well reefed and the headsail is not reefed.

Weather helm sometimes occurs when a helmsman, perhaps sailing single-handed, uses a mainsail only without any headsail.

Try a bigger rudder

A rudder that is too small sometimes causes excess weather helm.

Sail upright

Excess HEELING disturbs helm balance so sail your boat upright.

14. Learning to Sail: Stage Four— Advanced Techniques

Handling the gybe

(1) If the wind is strong and the water broken avoid an accidental gybe by *tacking down wind*. Sail with the wind well out on the quarter. Then turn into the wind and tack round on to the other gybe.
(2) Under storm conditions avoid even a deliberate gybe.
(3) When making a deliberate gybe warn the crew early. Time every movement and action so that they are made under full control.
(4) One of the most disconcerting things to happen during a gybe is to lose your sense of direction. This often happens because the helmsman has to handle both the mainsheet and tiller, watch the boom come over to the lee side and move himself across to the new weather side at one and the same time. Cross to the new weather side first while you are preparing to gybe then it is easier to see where the boat is heading and to correct the tiller.

Running goose-winged

When running with the wind dead aft or nearly aft a boat sometimes sails BY THE LEE with the wind on the wrong side of the mainsail. The headsail will probably set on the opposite side to the mainsail. This is known as sailing GOOSE-WINGED. A JIB POLE or WHISKER POLE is used to hold out the headsail. When the headsail first begins to draw on the opposite side this warns the helmsman he is sailing by the lee and must look out for an accidental gybe. It is bad practice to sail goose-winged in bad weather and broken water, especially when the boat begins to roll heavily.

Sailing goose-winged is the one occasion when the helmsman sits to leeward to steer, it gives him a good view ahead under the main boom. The helmsman is also in position for gybing. He need not worry about crossing over and only has to think about correcting the mainsheet and tiller.

The crew sit to windward and adjust the trim of the boat when gybing.

126

Rolling

When running with the wind aft boats tend to roll. Correct this by lowering the centre-plate a third of the way down. If this does not break the roll, sail on a broad reach with the wind over the quarter. The motion of a roll often makes the most hardened sailors feel unwell.

Rolling is not only uncomfortable, but also dangerous. A heavy lurch to windward may cause an accidental gybe, while a heavy roll to leeward may dip the main boom and swing the boat round by the lee with disastrous results.

Spinnaker handling

Ready to set

Stow the spinnaker in a bag or compartment so that it is all ready to set. Make sure there are no twists. It is a good plan to have the halyard, guy and sheet different colours. Check that they are secured to the three corners or clews of the sail ready for setting.

How to set

The spinnaker is set with the wind aft or nearly aft and the jib is often lowered. It is set opposite the mainsail with ropes attached to each of its three corners or clews. The sail is loose footed and is boomed out sideways, forward of the mast and shrouds. The boom is attached inboard to the mast and the tack of the spinnaker is fixed to the outer end of the boom. From this point a rope known as the SPINNAKER GUY leads aft to the cockpit of the boat and is used for setting and trimming the sail. This is the weather sheet. The lower corner of the sail or clew is inboard. The spinnaker sheet which is used for trimming the sail is attached to the clew and is the lee sheet. The spinnaker boom is sometimes fitted with a kicking strap to keep it down.

Hoisting the spinnaker

Once you have decided on which side of the boat to set the spinnaker, hoist quickly.

Attach the outboard end of the boom to the sail first and the inboard end of the boom second. Haul in the spinnaker guy so that the spinnaker boom is drawn aft about right angles to the fore-and-aft line of the boat. Belay the guy.

127

Trimming the sail

Use the spinnaker sheet for trimming the sail as you would a main-sheet. If the luff shakes or the sail collapses draw the sheet aft.

When cruising keep the spinnaker full by steering the boat to meet wind shifts. If you are racing and sailing on a strict course trim the sail with the spinnaker sheet and, if necessary, adjust the spinnaker guy.

Handing the spinnaker

HANDING is to haul down and stow the spinnaker. Ease the guy for'ard and spill the wind. Unship the boom at the mast end and draw it inboard. Release the sail at the outboard end of the boom. Lower the sail by easing the halyard. As the spinnaker is lowered it can become very unruly. Keep it under strict control. Gather the sail on to the foredeck or into the cockpit and keep it out of the water.

Sailing in light airs

Sailing well in light airs depends on having the proper equipment, how the boat is tuned and how she is handled.

Equipment

Use light sails cut full. If you have more than one suit of sails, they will be the largest. With light sails use light sheets, especially for headsails.

Use a Nylon burgee or cotton 'tellers' tied to the shrouds to tell you the direction of the lightest airs.

Tuning

A well-tuned boat has a clean bottom free from weed and barnacles and, if she is varnished, her bottom may even be polished. The bilges should be emptied of water and dry.

To get peak efficiency in light airs you may need to ease the shrouds a little and to tighten the leech line of the sail to make it fuller in the belly.

Handling

Watch the trim of the boat.

Movement of crew and helmsman should be 'catlike', tread light and no jerking.

Handle the sheets with a light touch and be gentle with the tiller.

128

When sailing to windward avoid 'pinching' too close to the wind. Sail her a little free. Some of the weight of the wind is used up in pressing the sails out to the correct angle against their sheets. By trimming the boat to leeward, thus letting gravity help the wind, you can save this extra bit of wind for more useful work.

Let the boat do the sailing. If there seems to be no wind always ease the sheets to find it, never pin them in.

Heavy weather sailing

Reefing
First practise reefing ashore or on your mooring and then when you are under sail in reasonable weather.

Tying reef points
Be sure you tie the reef pendants at the tack and clew before you tie the reef points. Start tying the reef points in the middle. If you are taking in more than one reef, start with the first one, tie all its points and complete the reef before starting on the second. Tie the points of alternate bands of reefs on alternate sides of the sails to prevent confusion when shaking the reefs out. Before hoisting sail make sure all the ties are complete. Before shaking out a reef see that the reef points are untied otherwise the sail may tear. Also make sure that the cringles of any reefs you are leaving in are secured by their pendants.

Roller reefing
Two suggestions for improving the set of your sail if roller reefing is used:

(1) As the boom is rolled pull the sail out at the clew end.
(2) Make and insert a light tapered wooden packing piece in the first fold of the sail at the after end of the boom as it rolls. This takes up the extra length of the leech and tops the boom. A drooping boom is dangerous because it may dip into the water and cause the boat to capsize.

With roller reefing the mainsheet sometimes gets twisted after turning the boom because the mainsheet attachment at the end of the boom turns round with the boom. If this happens sail up into the wind and twist the attachment in the opposite direction from the one in which you have been turning the boom.

129

Sailing in safety

CHECK=Safety

Safety depends on   C=Conditions
                         H=Handling
                         E=Equipment
                         C=Comfort
                         K=Knowledge

Conditions

Get forecasts of weather conditions from the BBC or Air Ministry and relate them to local weather.

If conditions become bad when you are sailing either get all sail off and proceed under oars or, if there is sea-room and the direction is right, continue under headsails only.

In bad conditions keep away from shallow water. In a blow, water is more disturbed over the shallows and if you go aground you may capsize and also break the centre-plate.

Avoid the lee shore.

Handling

Don't { Run with the wind *dead* aft.
Deliberately gybe in heavy weather.
Pinch to windward.
Luff into stays.
Make the mainsheet fast.

Do { Be alert for puffs and squalls and ease the sheets just before they come.
Look for smooth water when coming about.
Free the headsheets in heavy weather.
Keep the boat moving.

Equipment

Keep your boat equipment in good order.
See that the halyards can be released easily in an emergency.

Equip { Your boat with buoyancy and balers.
Yourself and the crew with life-jackets.
Your ditty bag with a knife and other tools for use in an emergency.

Comfort

Don't ⎰ Overload your boat, particularly in
heavy weather.
Over-estimate the power of your boat
to stand up to heavy seas.

Do ⎰ Keep your boat dry. If you take in water on
the windward leg bale out as soon as possible.
This is not only for comfort but will avoid the
danger of shifting water ballast and swamping.

Knowledge

Do ⎰ Know where you are going before you set off
and tell people ashore. Coastguards, customs
officers, harbourmasters and club officers are
always helpful. Give them your course,
destination and expected time of arrival.

Do ⎰ Know what to do in emergencies and work out
your scheme in advance for dealing with
jury rigs and other problems.

How to right a capsize

The boat should float

There should be enough buoyancy in the boat to let her float on her
side with the mast just in the water. The buoyancy should also be
sufficient to allow her to float when righted with the weight of one
crew on board and the water she will have taken in through the
centre-board case.

How to right her

The helmsman clambers on to the upturned side while the crew goes
into the water to windward and steps on to the centre-board. It may
be possible to right the boat immediately this way. If not, the mainsail
and headsail must be got down. Uncleat the halyards and haul down
the sails. If the halyards cannot be freed the crew will have to swim
round and unshackle the headboards. With the sail down, the crew
and helmsman to windward should be able to right the boat and as
she comes up the helmsman must clamber aboard quickly and balance
the swamped boat. Plug the top of the centre-board case with the

131

handful of cotton waste you keep in the ditty bag. Baling then starts and the crew eventually gets aboard again over the stern.

If it is impossible to right the capsized boat, the helmsman and the crew should sit on the upper side of the boat and wait for outside help. *Never leave a capsized boat*—it can be seen more easily than a man in the water and you will not get so exhausted sitting on the side as you would in the water.

Picking up a man overboard

To prevent this happening large boats are fitted with guard-rails. In small boats the crew may have a safety-belt and he should be wearing a life-jacket. Accidents do happen, however, and it is important to know instinctively what to do.

Action (1) Throw a life-jacket or a kapok cushion to hold.

          (2) Detail a look-out crew.

          (3) Gybe the boat deliberately *at once*.

          (4) Get look-out to direct you on to your objective.

          (5) Ease sheets and *take off way*.

          (6) Go alongside man overboard. When you gybe on to a man overboard you are invariably up to him within half a minute depending on the size of your boat.

If it is too rough to gybe you will have to put your boat about and sail back to the man overboard. This will take much longer.

As in all other branches of seamanship the only way to act instinctively and correctly is to practise under good conditions so that you are ready for the emergency when it happens. It is in any case good fun to practice with either a lifebuoy or on a fine summer day with a member of your crew, but make sure that there are other people about to help you when you practise this.

Heaving-to

If you want to make small adjustments to the rigging or other equipment try to do this on a reach and not head to wind. Head to wind you are out of control. Ease the sheets right away and slow down. To get under way again all you have to do is to haul in the mainsheet.

If you want to heave-to for some time, with a keel boat and with correctly balanced centre-board boats turn into the wind so that she is close-hauled. Sheet the jib to weather and ease the mainsheet. At

132

the same time put the tiller down slightly. The amount to ease the mainsheet and put the tiller down has to be found by experiment. The boat should lie quiet or sail ahead very gently.

Going aground and getting off

When you go aground you must think quickly:
(1) Is the tide rising or falling?
(2) Are you on a weather shore, a lee shore, or is the wind along the shore?

Keel boats

(1) **Falling tide.** You must get off *immediately*.

With the wind off-shore put the helm up hard, free the sheets and bear away. If this fails, get the crew overboard and push her round. Heel the boat to make her draw less water and the wind should blow you off.

(2) **Rising tide.** Put an anchor out in deeper water. You will be floated off as the tide rises and it does not matter even if you are on a lee shore.

Lee shore. Get all sail down at once. Heel the boat over as far as you can, if necessary by swinging the boom out and getting a hand 'to sit it out', pole off or rig oars and row off if you can. If this doesn't work in the first few minutes, and you have a dinghy, lay out a kedge anchor to windward and try to haul off. If the boat is still fast then rig LEGS at once to prevent the boat keeling over as she dries out. Make everything snug below and aloft, lay out the bower anchor at low water and wait till the tide re-floats her.

Dinghies

Rising or falling tide. It is of less importance to a dinghy whether the tide is rising or falling as the centre-plate can be raised to give more water.

Weather shore. If you go aground on a weather shore, free the sheet and as you bear away raise the centre-plate and you should be away.

Lee shore. Put the helm down immediately and let the headsails fly. If this brings you about, raise the centre-plate a little and sail away close-hauled.

133

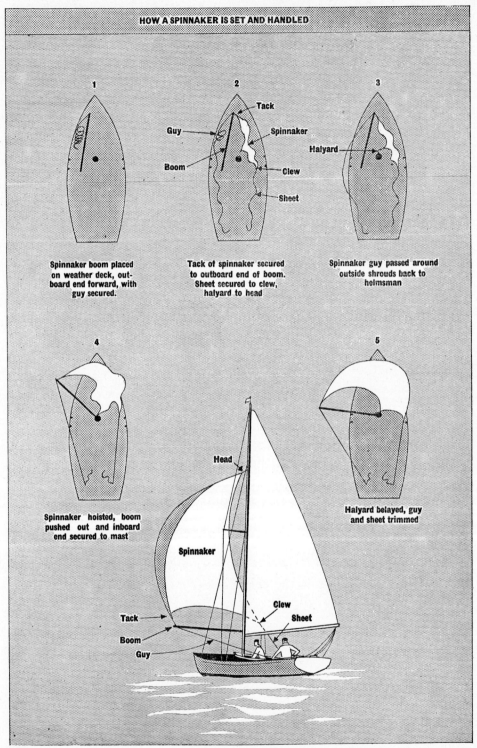

HOW A SPINNAKER IS SET AND HANDLED

1

Spinnaker boom placed on weather deck, outboard end forward, with guy secured.

2

Tack
Guy
Spinnaker
Boom
Clew
Sheet

Tack of spinnaker secured to outboard end of boom. Sheet secured to clew, halyard to head

3

Halyard

Spinnaker guy passed around outside shrouds back to helmsman

4

Spinnaker hoisted, boom pushed out and inboard end secured to mast

5

Halyard belayed, guy and sheet trimmed

Head
Spinnaker
Clew
Sheet
Tack
Boom
Guy

Never raise the centre-plate and try to sail on to windward in the hope of coming about. The boat makes more leeway before getting under way, she touches again and you are in a far worse predicament!

Gybing off a lee shore. It is possible to gybe off a lee shore when the wind is blowing fairly hard.

As you start to gybe, raise the centre-plate enough to give you water. Gybing will give you an abrupt turn which enables you to sail off quite fast.

Do not lift the centre-plate *before* gybing.

Falling tide. If you do not get off quickly, the water may become too shallow to get off at all. You must get the sails down, raise the centre-plate and row off or pull your way off with a kedge anchor. It may be necessary to rock the boat to free her, or even to lighten her by putting the crew overboard.

The best way of getting out of mud is the way you came in, i.e. backwards.

Why maintenance is important

It is as important to know how to look after a boat as it is to be able to sail her.

If she is properly maintained she will be safer when making a passage at sea, she will look better and sail better and she will keep her value.

When to do maintenance

From day to day when the boat is in commission.

During the winter when she is laid up.

Work at the end of the sailing season is known as LAYING UP, and in preparation for the following season, FITTING OUT.

A boat which is used a great deal may also need a MID-SEASON FIT OUT.

Maintenance includes work on:

(1) The hull.
(2) The standing and running rigging.
(3) The sails.
(4) Other gear.

The hull

How to reduce work

The amount of work to be done on the hull will be reduced:

IF the boat is sailed with care and not stranded, capsized or involved in collisions.

IF she is moored or anchored in clear water.

IF she is sailed with care alongside wharfs and jetties and protected by fenders.

IF the tender, should one be used to reach the boat on its moorings, has a permanent fender.

IF the launching trolley for a boat kept on shore is used with care and the boat is protected from the weather by a cover of waterproof canvas or strong plastic sheeting.

IF scars in the paintwork or varnish are touched up to avoid weathering of the bare wood.

IF barnacles and weed are regularly scrubbed off the boat's bottom with a hard brush or wooden scraper.

Laying up and fitting out the hull

This work is best carried out in a boat store under cover where you can keep tools and equipment, consumable materials like paint, varnish and thinners, and the boat's gear.

Warm weather and a dust-free atmosphere help the work and there must be the same meticulous care of brushes for all paintwork and varnishing.

Before laying up in the boat store clean off the barnacles immediately. They should never be allowed to dry on the hull otherwise your work will be twice as difficult. Hose down the inside of the boat to prevent mud from drying in.

Clinker- or carvel-built boats should not be left to dry out too much during the winter otherwise the planks may split. A canvas cover over the boat will prevent this, but a regular airing is needed to stop dry rot setting in. Alternatively, run the boat out into the rain every few weeks during the winter, if she can be shifted on a trolley.

Prepare for inspection

For a major refit, wash, scrub and clean the boat thoroughly before inspecting what has to be done.

Repairs to woodwork

All repairs to the woodwork must be done first. Inspect for split planks, broken timbers, soft or rotten patches and loose fastenings. Repairs should be done by a skilled boatbuilder but they can be tackled by an enthusiastic and well-informed amateur with specialized knowledge. Much depends on the type of boat construction involved. Repairs using fibreglass and epoxy resin have been well tried and tested and their use is recommended. Before attempting any repairs yourself learn as much as you can about the materials you intend to use.

Stripping paintwork

If the paintwork is flaking and bubbling it probably requires stripping. This is done with the aid of chemical strippers and scrapers such as

137

the 'Skarsten', or by using a blow-lamp but this needs care. If chemical strippers are used the woodwork must be neutralized afterwards by washing with white spirit and the stripping finished off with coarse sandpaper.

With proper care and re-painting a boat's paintwork should only require stripping to the bare wood about once in ten years. Normally when fitting out it is only necessary to rub down thoroughly with wet and dry paper, stop up all scars, apply one undercoat and one coat of marine enamel.

Re-painting

To re-paint from the bare wood start with a coat of priming paint with a red lead base, or a metallic primer. First rub down lightly. Then apply undercoats and rub down lightly between each undercoat with medium 'wet and dry paper' until a smooth surface is built up. Deep scars should be filled in with a proprietary brand of boat cement. The topsides of the hull are then finished off with a marine enamel.

All paints, varnishes and stopping materials should be marine grade and produced by firms who specialize in marine paints and varnishes.

Anti-fouling

If only the topsides are enamelled the boat's bottom may require special ANTI-FOULING PAINT which hinders the growth of barnacles and weed. Anti-fouling paint is not usually thinned and is applied only a few hours before launching. Hard racing copper anti-fouling is recommended as it does not wear off so easily when the boat's bottom is scrubbed.

Quantities for re-painting

A 14-foot boat requires about ½ pint of topside enamel, 1 pint of undercoat, 1 pint of anti-fouling, and 1 pint of varnish for her annual refit.

The rigging

This includes standing and running rigging, i.e. the wire rope, cordage and fittings.

When laying up, thoroughly inspect the rigging and order replacements. Rigging must be fit for the job and doubtful items discarded.

Never postpone the renewal of rigging that is the worse for wear. A breakage under way may be costly and highly dangerous.

Wire rope
Inspection. If the galvanizing has worn or disappeared from the wire rope, brush away the surface rust with a wire brush. Prickly ends along a wire will show that the strands are breaking and it is past its best. Bend the wire sharply at right angles and if it is still good it should spring back to a straight line. If it does not it should be discarded.

Replacement. When measuring for new wire it is worth remembering that wire rope stretches. Although stainless wire is more expensive initially it is a very sound investment in the long run. Wire splicing should be done professionally.

Stowing. When laying up and fitting out, oil the wire rope with an oily rag saturated with linseed oil. When stowing the wire rigging coil down properly to avoid kinks, sharp bends or nips and label each item clearly. At the same time grease all shackles, rigging screws, and blocks involved.

Cordage
Inspection. Inspect cordage for rot, mildew, damp and chafe. Open up the strands in several places by twisting against the lay to see the inside. Rot shows up as grey dust and broken fibres, dampness by dark discoloration of the fibres and mildew by a light grey film of dust. Chafe shows up by the worn character of the outside of the rope.

Replacement. Foresheets wear most quickly and must be renewed at least every season. The mainsheet will often serve for two seasons. The service you obtain from any rope will vary very much according to the number of hours it has actually worked in a season and upon the material from which the rope is made. BRAIDED COTTON or ROUND SENNIT is always to be treated as doubtful after a season because its interior cannot be inspected and it retains moisture more readily and rots more easily and quickly. A doubtful rope can then be tested by using a PROOF LOAD and renewed if there is any sign of failure.

139

Stowing. Cordage should be stowed in a cool, well-ventilated, dry place. It should be free of salt and moisture. If ever stowed when wet bring it out for drying as soon as possible. Always see that the ends are finished off properly with whippings and that the coils are made up properly. When laying up, cordage should be washed, rinsed and dried thoroughly, then coiled and labelled before storing away.

Turning. Sometimes the worn or chafed parts of halyards and sheets can be safely dealt with by turning the halyards and sheets end for end.

Sails

Day-to-day care

Sails will last much longer and remain efficient by correct day-to-day usage. Take care in bending on your sails and setting them and in trimming them correctly when under way. Look carefully at the setting of your sails when reefed.

When the sails get wet while you are out sailing, ease the halyards and the ties that secure the sails at the clew and the peak, if the sail is a gaff or gunter. This prevents distortion when the sailcloth and rope shrink with the wet. After sailing in heavy weather the sails will be wet with salt water and will need rinsing in fresh water to remove the salt. Accumulated salt makes the sails hard like a board. They will be inefficient in light airs because they set less well. Avoid letting the sails FRAP, i.e. shake unnecessarily. When you have reached your mooring or the shore, or a river bank and you are not actually sailing, lower the sails as soon as possible. Avoid chafe on the sails when under way. See that the lee backstay is always clear. When running before the wind see if the sail is pressing against any rigging aloft and if it is fit the rigging with protective pads or BAGGY WRINKLES.

If you leave your sails bent to the spars for the season, when you come in after sailing slacken off lashings at the clew of the mainsail and the peak, furl them carefully and use a sail cover. Sails left on the spars should be proofed against water and mildew by a sailmaker. Proofing is a good thing for all cotton sails because cotton is easily attacked by mildew if there is any dampness and this leads to rot.

Sails that are bent to their spars with a track and track hanks, or by a grooved spar and bolt rope should always be taken off and stowed each time you finish sailing and come ashore.

Sails should be stowed in a sail-bag or sail-locker and must never

140

be put away wet. Repairs to sails should always have immediate attention and sails should be inspected regularly and carefully for weak points that are developing.

Laying up

At the end of the season go carefully over every seam to look for stitching that is broken or coming undone. Look for small holes carefully and examine the seizings of any metal track or piston hanks that may be fitted. Major repairs and alterations should be done by a sailmaker.

The sails should be soaked and washed thoroughly in fresh water, dried carefully and stowed away in a cool dry place free from vermin.

Stretching new sails

It is most important to know how to care for a new sail. This is known as STRETCHING the sail.

New cotton sails need stretching for about 12 to 18 hours of easy sailing.

Sails should only be stretched in fine weather with a *gentle* breeze. Strong winds are harmful at this stage and a new sail should never be reefed until it has been properly stretched.

Bend on the sails with the luff rope and foot rope hand-taut so that the wrinkles in the sailcloth are only just pulled out. After an hour's sailing alter the set of the sails by hauling a little more on the halyard and on the foot rope.

A foresail with a wire luff stands much harder treatment from the start because the wire luff cannot be overstretched or distorted.

When the helmsman is stretching the sails he aims at obtaining the best possible aerofoil shape in the new sail, by quietly stretching them inch by inch.

Choose if possible a reaching course and avoid sailing close-hauled.

Do not wash the sails until they have been stretched.

Other gear

(1) When laying-up, inspect and oil all working parts such as sheaves and blocks, rudder gudgeons and pintles and the centre-board winch.

141

(2) Examine the anchor and its warp, and any spare cordage which has been carried aboard.

(3) Check the balers, water pump, life-jackets and any tools you carry aboard and oil them lightly.

(4) Look carefully at toe-straps and renew if they are at all worn. Examine the burgee and its fittings, the kicking strap and the launching trolley.

New Materials

New materials are continually being introduced in the construction of the hull and all the boat's gear and normally their care and maintenance is different. One or two features are mentioned here as illustrations.

Paints and varnishes. New paints and varnishes based on polyester and epoxy resins are being introduced. They are extremely durable and hard-wearing and they will probably last much longer. Pay special attention to the maker's instructions for application and maintenance.

Sailcloth and cordage. New synthetic fibres like 'Terylene' have new characteristics and need different care and maintenance from traditional materials. The manufacturers and sailmakers will give advice on their handling.

Deck finishes. Plastic sheeting and rubber or synthetic rubber sheeting may be used instead of canvas and paint or varnish or instead of the laid deck. The former last longer and reduce the work of looking after your boat to a marked degree.

Glass fibre and epoxy resin glue used in hull construction and repair may be self-coloured and require no painting or further protection.

Nylon or other synthetic boat fittings, e.g. sheaves and blocks, bushes, cleats and balers. Life-jackets and personal clothing are also produced in these new materials.

Such rapid progress is being made in the production of new materials that the whole field of traditional boat maintenance is now changing.

16. The Rule of the Road at Sea—I

A motorist is not allowed to drive a car unless he knows the Highway Code and a helmsman should not sail a boat until he has learnt the Rule of the Road at Sea which is given in the Thirty-one Articles of International Regulations for Preventing Collisions at Sea. Anyone who takes charge of a commercial vessel has to memorize each Article by heart. Although this is not necessary for a small boat sailor, he should understand the rules and know how to apply them. He may never command a great liner but if there is one about he must know what she is going to do so that he can decide on the proper course of action for his own boat.

In this chapter and the following chapter the Rules are grouped and discussed in an order which should help the reader to learn their content so that he can deal with any situation which he may meet at sea.

Before learning the Rule of the Road Under Sail it is important to revise the Points of Sailing learnt in Chapter 7. This chapter therefore begins with revisions, followed by the Seven Rules which apply under sail and a note on how to interpret them. In addition to the special rules for sailing boats there are certain Steering Rules to be learnt which apply to all vessels and must be obeyed equally by the small boat sailor and the man in command of an ocean-going liner. The one object is to reduce the risk of collision by making sure that men in charge of vessels all take the correct action. There are also a number of main Steering Rules for Power Driven vessels which are included, together with lists of vessels which both sailing and power-driven craft must avoid.

At this stage it is important to know the Sound Signals which are used when vessels are visible to each other, although the sound signals which apply by night or in thick weather are dealt with in the next chapter.

It is possible that there will be important changes in the near future to the rules that govern the 'right of way' of sailing boats. Some recommendations are given on pages 179 and 180.

Finally, as an aid to learning, the rules for sailing ships are summarized in verse (see page 152).

Revision of points of sailing and port and starboard tacks

(1) The difference between being **close-hauled** and **with the wind free.**

(2) The difference between **port** and **starboard tacks.** Most of the sailing rules are bound up with understanding these definitions and what they mean in practice.

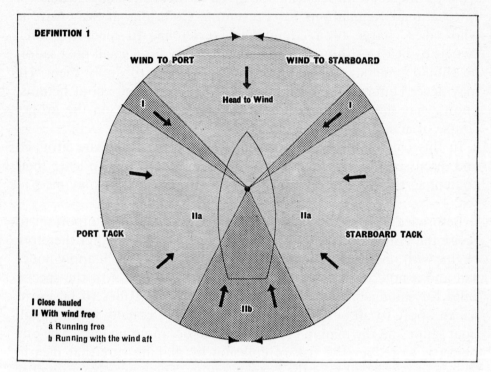

DEFINITION 1

WIND TO PORT   WIND TO STARBOARD

Head to Wind

I   I

IIa   IIa

PORT TACK   STARBOARD TACK

IIb

I Close hauled
II With wind free
   a Running free
   b Running with the wind aft

(1) Close-hauled and with the wind free

A boat is sailing CLOSE-HAULED when she is sailing against the wind, i.e. into the wind. The headsail is trimmed close inboard and the mainsail boom is hauled close in to the boat's quarter.

If a boat is sailing with the wind and sails in any position other than CLOSE-HAULED then she is sailing WITH THE WIND FREE. With the wind free a boat can be sailing in two positions: (1) RUNNING FREE and (2) RUNNING WITH THE WIND AFT. The regulations differentiate between the two cases, and the rules for each case are different.

RUNNING FREE is what most yachtsmen know as 'reaching'. If the wind is coming from abeam, or even slightly forward of it, she is running free. If the wind is anywhere aft of the beam she is still running

144

free until the wind draws aft of about two points on the quarter, when she is then said to be RUNNING WITH THE WIND AFT. The rules make a special case of a boat with the 'wind aft', and this applies also if the wind is slightly out on either quarter.

A boat is RUNNING WITH THE WIND AFT when the wind is following the boat. The boat is literally being blown along, and the headsail and mainsail boom are sheeted right off so that they make an angle of nearly 90 degrees with the boat's fore-and-aft line.

(2) **Port and starboard tacks**

When the boom and mainsail are on the starboard side, whether the boat is with the wind free or close-hauled, she is said to be on the PORT TACK. The wind is coming from over the port side of the boat.

When the boom and mainsail are on the port side, whether the boat is with the wind free or close-hauled, she is said to be on the STAR-BOARD TACK. The wind is coming from over the starboard side of the boat.

The diagrams summarize these positions of sailing in relation to the wind direction and to the rule of the road under sail.

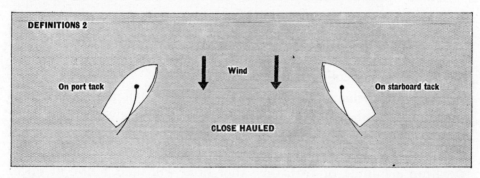

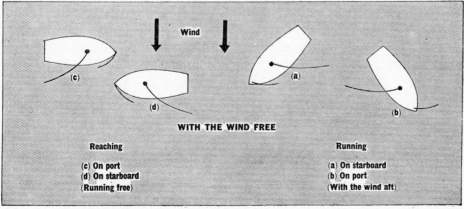

The rule of the road under sail*

The **rules** may be interpreted as follows:

(1) Boats that are CLOSE-HAULED have right of way over those with the wind free.

(2) When two boats are close-hauled the one on STARBOARD TACK has right of way.

(3) When two boats have the wind free the one with the boom over the port side, i.e. on STARBOARD TACK has right of way.

(4) The boat WITH THE WIND AFT keeps clear.

(5) It is customary and courteous for the WINDWARD BOAT TO KEEP CLEAR OF THE BOAT TO LEEWARD. The windward boat is the one on the side from which the wind is blowing. The reason for the rule is that it is generally difficult for the leeward boat to work up to windward, but the windward boat can run down to leeward easily and so has greater freedom of action. The actual law states: 'When the two boats are running free the windward boat keeps clear', but good seamanship makes this apply to close-hauled boats as well.

(6) Whichever the point of sailing the OVERTAKING BOAT keeps clear.

(7) POWER gives way to SAIL.

How to interpret Sailing Rules

(1) **Risk of collision.** When vessels large or small are about their ordinary business, 'if the bearing does not change very much there is risk of collision'. It is assumed that as soon as there is *risk*, the vessels will alter course. If the 'give away' vessel does not act within a minute or two, the other boat will take action at once, long before the *risk* becomes *danger* and while there is still plenty of sea-room.

(2) **Danger of collision.** Boats are presumed to be in danger of collision when they are within three boat-lengths of each other, the larger boat to count. The rules must be applied at once. Always keep a sharp look-out. Try to think what the other boat will do. Obey the rules as set out above; make your decision and ACT EARLY, at the latest when you come within range of being in danger of collision, and BOLDLY. A bold alteration of course helps the crew on the other boat to see what you are doing.

* See Appendix on page 179.

RULE OF THE ROAD FOR BOATS UNDER SAIL

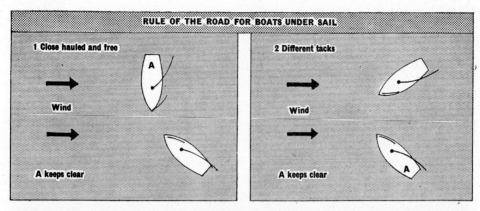

1 Close hauled and free

Wind

A keeps clear

2 Different tacks

Wind

A keeps clear

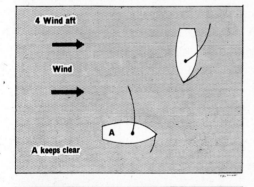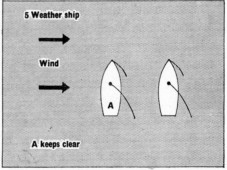

3   Case 1   Different tacks   Case 2

Wind

A keeps clear

Wind

A keeps clear

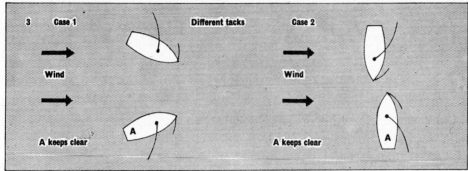

4 Wind aft

Wind

A keeps clear

5 Weather ship

Wind

A keeps clear

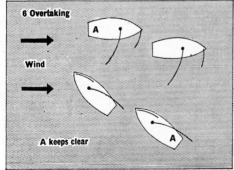

6 Overtaking

Wind

A keeps clear

7 Commercial craft

147

(3) Be cautious of the boat running with the wind aft although she is obliged to keep clear. To avoid you she may have to gybe in a heavy sea and expose herself to serious danger. This rule is a relic of the days of square-rigged sailing ships. In those days it was very difficult to sail to windward, i.e. to sail close-hauled. The boat running with the wind aft was much easier to manoeuvre and was thus required to give way. Today the boat close-hauled is much more under control than the boat running with the wind aft, so that if you are cruising and not racing, consider carefully the position of the boat approaching you and her possible difficulties.

(4) Although it is the duty of power craft to keep clear it is wiser not to take this rule too much for granted. Users of commercial vessels are professional sailors and they are most courteous and understanding. They know the rules as professionals and will invariably do the right thing. Return this good will and treat them generously. Remember commercial vessels normally draw a lot of water, (i.e. their draught is great) and they require room to manoeuvre and even to stop. They are often working to a definite schedule with little time to spare, so that if you meet a tanker or cargo vessel in restricted waters, such as a river or an estuary, do not force her to take costly avoiding action unnecessarily. Be gracious and understanding and keep out of her way. To avoid confusion alter your course boldly and in plenty of time.

(5) It is well to remember that each skipper is responsible for the safety of his own ship; that no one should take charge of a watch at sea unless he has a thorough knowledge of the Regulations for Preventing Collisions at Sea; and that when the rules require one vessel to keep out of the way, the other is expected to keep her course and speed.

(6) If you are out cruising and you meet a number of boats racing, you may have right of way but it is customary to give them a clear passage.

Steering rules

For all vessels

(1) If the bearing of an approaching vessel does not change very much, it must be presumed that there is risk of collision.

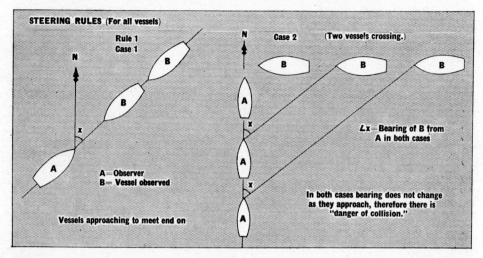

(2) If of two vessels approaching each other one is much more manoeuvrable than the other, the former is required to keep out of the way.

(3) A vessel which has to keep out of the way must never cross ahead of the other.

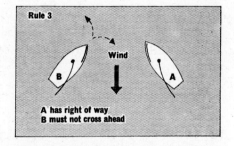

(4) A vessel which has to keep out of the way must do so in good time, and indicate her intention by a bold alteration of course.

(5) The vessel with right of way must keep her course and speed.

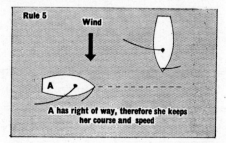

In order to avoid immediate danger vessels may depart from these rules and the boat with right of way may decide to give way. For example if, in thick weather, a vessel found herself so close to another that a collision could not be avoided by the action alone of the vessel which has to give way, the boat with right of way must also take action. On another occasion, as suggested above, it is wise for the small boat sailor, even if his boat has right of way, to keep clear of commercial vessels in restricted waters.

For steam vessels

Steam vessel is the term used in the 31 Articles to cover any power-driven vessel.

STEERING RULES FOR STEAM VESSELS

(1) Approaching each other in narrow channels they should keep to the right.

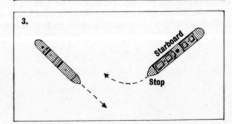

(2) Meeting end-on, which implies the vessels have come from opposite directions, they should both alter course to starboard, i.e. to the right.

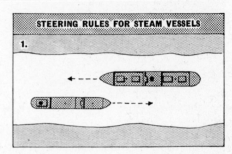

(3) Crossing each other, the one with the other on her starboard side should keep out of the way.

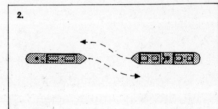

(4) The power-driven vessel which has to give way to another vessel shall on approaching her slacken speed, stop or reverse.

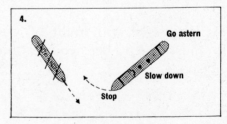

Boats which keep out of the way

A sailing boat keeps out of the way of:

(1) Any vessel she is overtaking.

(2) Any vessel that is fishing, towing or cable-laying or is less manoeuvrable.

(3) Other sailing vessels when the rules require her to do so.

A power-driven vessel keeps out of the way of:

(1) A sailing vessel.

(2) A vessel she is overtaking.

(3) A vessel that is not manoeuvrable, such as a boat with steering or engine trouble, or a boat that is fishing or towing.

(4) Other power-driven vessels where the rules require her to do so. *When two power craft are under way and would cross one another, the vessel which has the other on her starboard side keeps clear.*

Yacht racing rules 1959

Right-of-way section

(1) Opposite tack rules: When two boats are on opposite tacks, the port tack keeps clear.

(2) Same tack rules: When two boats are on the same tack the over-taking yacht/boat keeps clear and if neither yacht is overtaking the windward yacht/boat keeps clear.

A boat is on a tack unless coming about or gybing. The term wind-ward yacht or boat applies only to yachts that overlap, i.e. when neither is clear astern.

These rules are far simpler than those of Article 17 of the 31 Articles* and any element of doubt as to which rule to apply is removed. There are other rules but they apply to the special circumstances of racing.

* Exactly the same as the proposed new Articles (1960). See Appendix, page 179.

Thomas Gray's lines or aids to memory*

Now these four rules† we all must note
Are no use in a sailing boat,
For when we're driven by the wind,
A different set of rules we'll find.

A close-hauled ship you'll never see,
Give way to one that's running free,
It's easier running free to steer
And that's the reason she keeps clear.

Both ships close-hauled or both quite free
On different tacks we all agree,
The ship which has the wind to port
Must keep well clear is what we're taught.

With wind the same side you will see
One ship's to windward, one's to lee,
The leeward ship goes right ahead,
The weather one gives way instead.

At other times the altering craft
Is that which has the wind right aft.

Lucke's Rules

A power boat must never fail
to alter course for those who sail.

A ship with net or dredge or trawl
May do no more than barely crawl
A *seaman* to himself will say,
'This vessel's hampered. I'll give way.'

No matter what the rules may say
The overtaking ship gives way.

These cover the most important rules for cases which do not come
under rules of Steamships or rules for sailing-ships because they apply
to both types.

* Thomas Gray's aids to memory as applied to sailing craft are to be discontinued as soon as
the Appendix becomes law (see page 180).

† Four rules refers to Gray's lines on the steering of steam vessels by night. See page 156.

17. Rule of the Road—II

Terms to show what boats are doing

In understanding the rule of the road by day and by night it is essential to remember the terms which show what boats are doing.

A boat is:

At anchor or on a mooring when secured to the sea-bed or shore by a warp or chain attached to an anchor or mooring.

Under way when a vessel is not at anchor, made fast to the shore or aground.

Not under command when she is under way but not under full control, that is, not manoeuvrable. She may have just been detached from her anchor or mooring or she may be drifting with her engines out of action, her steering gear broken or be dismasted.

Making way when she is moving ahead or astern. This is sometimes confused with the term 'under way', but a boat can be under way although she is not necessarily making way.

Special vessels are vessels which in general are not very manoeuvrable, fishing vessels at work, vessels towing and being towed, pilot vessels and vessels that are cable laying or dredging. They are the hampered vessels and *all others must keep clear of them.* By night they may be recognized by the special pattern and character of their lights.

How vessels are recognized at night—Light Signals

Vessels are recognized at night by the lights they carry. This is regulated by the 31 Articles. To take charge of a watch at night you must know the pattern of the navigation lights illustrated on page 154. More detailed information is given in Table 1.

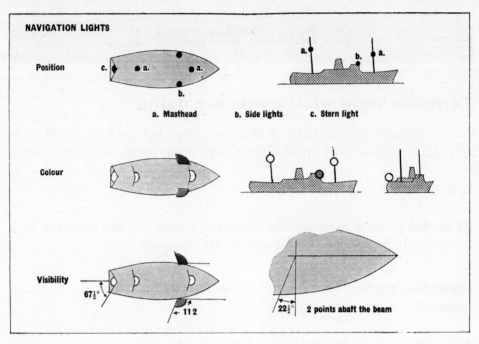

NAVIGATION LIGHTS

Position

c.   a.   b.

a. Masthead   b. Side lights   c. Stern light

Colour

Visibility

67½°

← 112

22½°   2 points abaft the beam

Table 1   How to recognize vessels at night

KIND OF VESSEL	NAVIGATION LIGHTS CARRIED	COLOUR OF LIGHTS	POSITION FROM WHICH THEY ARE VISIBLE	DISTANCE VISIBLE
Steam vessels **Under 40 tons**	1 masthead	White	Right ahead to 2 points (22½ degrees) abaft the beam on both sides	3 miles
	2 side lights	Port—red Starboard— green	Right ahead to 2 points (22½ degrees) abaft the beam on each side	1 mile
	1 stern light	White	Right aft to 6 points (67½ degrees) on each side of a vessel	1 mile
Over 40 tons	2 masthead	White	Right ahead to 2 points (22½ degrees) abaft the beam on both sides	5 miles
	2 side lights	Port—red Starboard— green	Right ahead to 2 points (22½ degrees) abaft the beam on each side	2 miles
	1 stern light	White	Right aft to 6 points (67½ degrees) on each side of vessel	1 mile

KIND OF VESSEL	NAVIGATION LIGHTS CARRIED	COLOUR OF LIGHTS	POSITION FROM WHICH THEY ARE VISIBLE	DISTANCE VISIBLE
Sailing vessels	2 side lights	Port—red Starboard— green	Right ahead to 2 points ($22\frac{1}{2}$ degrees) abaft the beam on each side	2 miles
	1 stern light	White	Right aft to 6 points ($67\frac{1}{2}$ degrees) on each side of vessel	2 miles
Vessels of less than 20 tons under sails or oars	Sidelights or lantern which has green glass on one side and red on the other	Port—red Starboard— green	Right ahead to 2 points abaft the beam on each side	1 mile
Vessels at anchor Under 150 feet in length	1 riding light on forestay	White	All round	2 miles
Over 150 feet in length	A second light right aft. (The first not less than 20 feet above deck and the second 15 feet lower)	White	All round	3 miles
Vessel not under command If she is not making way	2 lights—forward	Red (black ball shapes by day)	All round	2 miles
If she is making way	2 side lights in addition	Port—red Starboard— green	Light ahead to 2 points ($22\frac{1}{2}$ degrees) abaft the beam on each side.	2 miles
Special vessels	Special pattern	Different from any of the above		

Unless you recognize a vessel's lights and can apply the rule of the road, give her right of way without question and keep clear for she is probably a special vessel.

From the pattern and colour of the ship's lights it is possible to tell:

(1) Whether she is anchored or under way.

(2) Whether a ship is under power or under sail.

(3) If under sail which tack she is on.

(4) Her course and direction—approaching, crossing or receding.

(5) Whether she is under full control or disabled.

(6) In special cases what job she is doing.

This information, which is illustrated on page 156, helps the sailor to apply THE RIGHT OF WAY RULES by night.

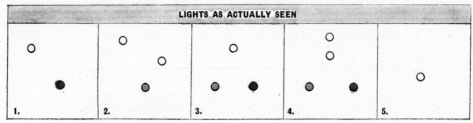

LIGHTS AS ACTUALLY SEEN

1. Small steam vessels crossing from right to left   2. Large steam vessels crossing from left to right
3 and 4. Steam vessels approaching   5. Most often, steam vessels receding or at anchor.
Sailing vessels, 1 and 2, without the white light

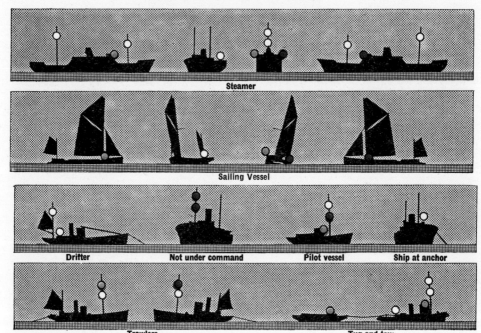

Steamer

Sailing Vessel

Drifter   Not under command   Pilot vessel   Ship at anchor

Trawlers   Tug and tow

Collisions

If a collision occurs, as far as he is able, the skipper of each vessel must render assistance to the other.

Thomas Gray's lines or aids to memory

These are in the form of a short poem and presume a knowledge of the navigation lights.

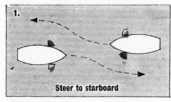

Steer to starboard

TWO VESSELS MEETING

1 When both lights you see ahead,
   Steer to starboard, show your RED.

156

TWO VESSELS PASSING

2 Green to green or red to red,
   Perfect safety, go ahead.

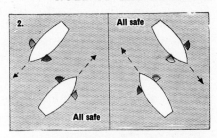

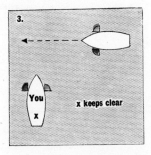

TWO VESSELS
CROSSING

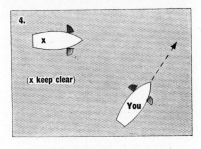

3 If to your starboard red appears,
   It is your duty to keep clear,
   To act as judgment says is proper,
   To port or starboard, back or stop her.

4 If on your port is seen
   A steamer's starboard light of green
   Nothing much for you to do
   For green to port keeps clear of you.

Sound signals

Like the motor vehicle on the road, the ship at sea and on inland waterways is equipped to make sound signals. Unlike those of the motor vehicle, the sound signals made by ships conform to a regular pattern.

Steam vessels use whistles or sirens; sailing vessels should use foghorns.

A long blast should last from four to six seconds; a short blast for one second.

Vessels visible to each other

When approaching each other, and visible to each other, vessels altering course in relation to the 31 Articles must indicate their action as follows:

I am directing my course to STARBOARD—ONE SHORT BLAST
I am directing my course to PORT—TWO SHORT BLASTS
My engines are going FULL SPEED ASTERN—THREE SHORT
BLASTS

It is worth repeating that these signals are to be given only when

157

vessels are in sight of one another. Sound signals of this kind given in fog only add to the confusion.

In thick weather

These only apply when vessels are not visible to each other. They show, as far as possible, that boats are near to each other, and their approximate position.

Table 2 **Sound signals in thick weather**

KIND OF VESSEL	METHOD OF SIGNALLING	FREQUENCY
Sailing vessels		At intervals of:
Under way: starboard tack	1 blast	1 min.
Under way: port tack	2 blasts	1 min.
Under way: running free	3 blasts	1 min.
Steam vessels		
Under way	1 prolonged blast	2 mins.
Under way but stopped	2 prolonged blasts	2 mins.
Vessels at anchor		
Under 350 feet long	Ring bell vigorously for 5 seconds	1 min.
Over 350 feet long	In addition beat a gong at stern	
Vessel towing	1 long blast and 2 short blasts	2 mins.
Vessel towed	1 long blast and 3 short blasts	2 mins.
Fishing vessel	1 short blast and ring bell	1 min.

Special signals

(1) Letter U ·· — 'You are standing into danger.'
(2) Letter R · — · 'The way is off my ship, you may feel your way past me.'
(3) Letter V ··· — 'I require assistance.'
(4) Letter K — · — 'Stop immediately.'

May be given by flash or sound from ships and lighthouses.

18. The Buoyage System

While sailors navigate on the open seas and oceans by solar and stellar observations, wireless bearings and radar, and in coastal areas by taking bearings on features which are clearly visible on the coast and marked on the map, they need more detailed information to negotiate the shallows and shoals and to avoid dangers and obstructions when sailing close inshore or approaching an estuary or harbour.

What are buoys?

(1) They are floating objects moored to the sea-bed.

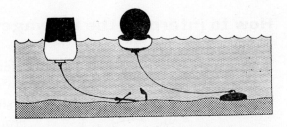

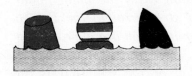

(2) They have a definite shape and colour so that sailors may see and recognize them from some distance away.

(3) Some buoys have topmarks fitted which tell you whether you are at the inner or outer end of a channel.

Topmark

A light

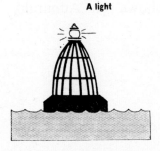

(4) Many buoys have lights, bells or whistles attached to show their position in darkness and in thick weather. Recently some buoys have been fitted with radar reflectors so that they can be picked out with modern navigational aids.

Are buoys the same everywhere?
An international system, known as the lateral system, was introduced in 1937. Not all areas have been converted to it and there are still local variations. The Admiralty Sailing Directions describe and show

the variations in any particular area. The less important channels and small ports are sometimes marked with stakes or withies. Inland waters or rivers are frequently marked with posts painted the appropriate colour.

Why is the buoyage system necessary?
Buoys are the signposts of the sea—the sea-marks used by sailors when making coastal passages and entering port. They are used to mark fairways and channels, shoals and banks, rocks, wrecks and other obstructions to a safe passage, and they supplement the work of lightships and lighthouses.

How to interpret the buoyage system

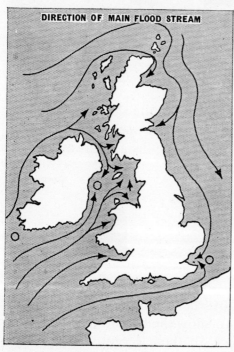

DIRECTION OF MAIN FLOOD STREAM

Tidal flow round British Isles
To read and apply the buoyage system correctly, *assume you are proceeding with the main flood-tide or stream round the British Isles or that you are approaching a port, river or estuary from the direction of the sea,* that is, in the direction of the flood-tide.

The general direction of the tidal flow round the British Isles is shown in the map. Detailed information for particular areas is shown on Admiralty charts.

Main channel buoys
When you are sailing in the same direction as the main flood-tide you will find that:

The right-hand side of the channel which is the starboard hand is marked with STARBOARD HAND BUOYS coloured BLACK or BLACK AND WHITE CHEQUERED. They are CONICAL in shape and may have topmarks and lights.

160

The left-hand side of the channel which is the port hand is marked with PORT HAND BUOYS coloured RED or RED AND WHITE CHEQUERED. They are cylindrical or CAN-shaped and may also have topmarks and lights.

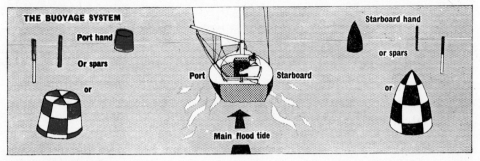

Numbered buoys

Buoys are numbered from the seaward end starting *one to port* and *two to starboard*. Odd numbers are all to port and even numbers all to starboard.

Wreck buoys

WRECK BUOYS show the position of wrecks dangerous to shipping.

They are painted GREEN with the word WRECK in white.

They may have three shapes indicating on which hand to leave the wreck when proceeding with the main flood or in from seaward to shoreward.

CONICAL . . .	leave to STARBOARD
CAN	leave to PORT
SPHERICAL . .	pass on EITHER HAND

A wreck may also be shown by a WRECK MARKING VESSEL. The side to pass is shown by lights or shapes in the yard-arm as illustrated.

Give wreck buoys a very clear berth and in light airs be very careful that the tide does not carry you down on to the wreck.

Middle ground buoys

MIDDLE GROUND BUOYS mark the inner and outer ends of a shoal or obstruction in a channel. They may also mark the point where a channel divides into two. They may be passed on either side.

Middle ground buoys are SPHERICAL in shape and coloured with BLACK AND WHITE or RED AND WHITE HORIZONTAL STRIPES.

A topmark indicates whether they are inner or outer buoys and the colour shows on which side the main channel lies. If the stripes are red and white the main channel is to starboard and if black and white it is to port. A special topmark shows when the channels are of equal importance.

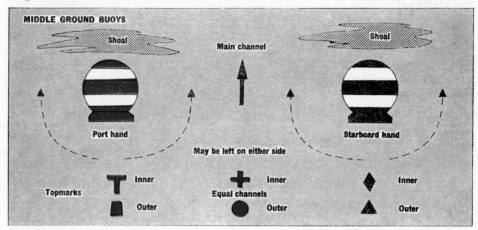

Mid-channel buoys

MID-CHANNEL BUOYS show the middle of a main channel or fairway.

They may be of ANY SHAPE except cone, can or sphere. The colour is BLACK AND WHITE or RED AND WHITE VERTICAL STRIPES. This latter is a most important distinguishing feature.

Always leave mid-channel buoys to port whatever the direction of the main flood and whether you are sailing seaward or towards the coast because it is the rule of the road that in restricted channels for two-way traffic you should always keep to the right.

Special buoys

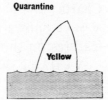

Quarantine

Yellow

(1) **Quarantine buoys**—mark anchorages for vessels waiting for permission from port authorities or H.M. Customs to enter harbour. They may be of ANY SHAPE but are YELLOW in colour.

Spoil ground

Yellow

(2) **Spoil ground buoys**—show where dredgers or barges may drop their refuse. They may be of ANY SHAPE but the colour is distinctive—BLACK AND YELLOW VERTICAL STRIPES. They may also be used to mark sewer outfalls.

Telegraph

(3) **Cable buoys**—show the position of any cables and prohibit anchoring in the area. They may be of ANY SHAPE, BLACK in colour with the word TELEGRAPH painted in WHITE.

Isolated danger

(4) **Isolated danger buoys** are SPHERICAL in shape and they have RED, WHITE AND BLACK HORIZONTAL STRIPES.

Leading marks

Features on shore which are easily seen and recognized, beacons and lighthouses are sometimes shown on charts and in sailing instructions as LEADING MARKS if, by keeping them in line, you are able to sail a course in safe and navigable channels.

TYPICAL LEADING MARKS

163

Charts

A MAP shows the outline of the coast, the height of the land and features on shore like roads, railways and buildings.

A CHART shows the outline of the shoreline, and the depth of the sea below low water level. Low water level is the level below which the tide seldom falls and is known as the CHART DATUM. The chart therefore shows the minimum depth of water. The depths are shown in fathoms and in shallow water in fathoms plus feet thus 3/4 equals three fathoms four feet at low water. The feet figure in mixed depths is always given in smaller type. Depths are often in feet in harbour charts. The title escutcheon of a chart always includes the words SOUNDINGS IN FEET or SOUNDINGS IN FATHOMS in block letters. Look for this before using the chart.

The height of shoals which are regularly uncovered by the tide is shown in feet, thus 4 equals 4 feet above chart datum.

Charts also show the buoyage system, using the symbols illustrated, the nature of the sea-bed using a standard system of conventional signs, the lightships and lighthouses round our coasts and how buoys are lighted.

HOW CHARTS SHOW BUOYS

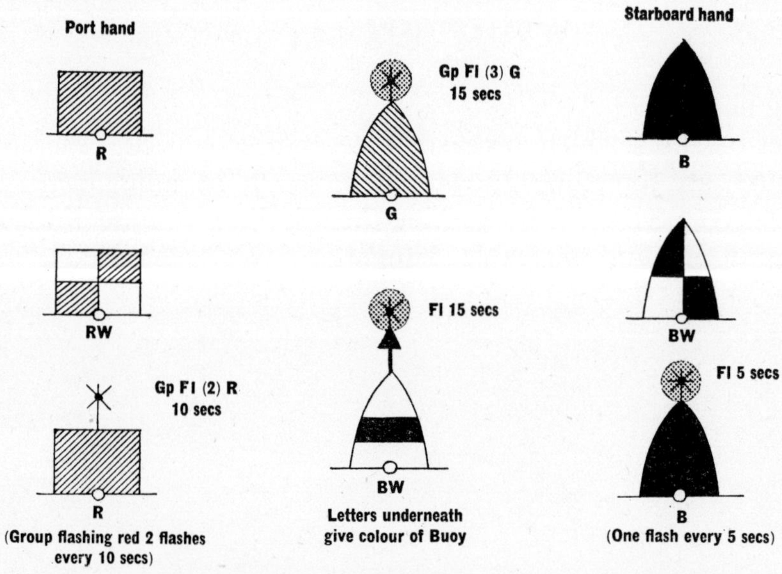

Port hand

Starboard hand

Gp Fl (3) G
15 secs

R

G

B

RW

Fl 15 secs

BW

Gp Fl (2) R
10 secs

Fl 5 secs

R
(Group flashing red 2 flashes
every 10 secs)

BW
Letters underneath
give colour of Buoy

B
(One flash every 5 secs)

Lights indicated in letter code, e.g. Gp Fl (3) G 15 secs = A group flashing 3 flashes then interval of
darkness 15 secs from first flash to first in next group

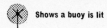 Shows a buoy is lit

Lights

Even if you are only a dinghy sailor and you do not intend to sail by night you may have to in an emergency. This is why it is advisable to know how buoys are lit, how to recognize the combinations of lights and how they are marked on a chart. The characteristics of the lights and the names given to them are shown in the accompanying table, and the method by which they are shown on a chart is also indicated.

Stationary lights by night and how they are marked on a chart

DESCRIPTION	CHARACTER	CHART SYMBOL
A flashing light	Regular series of flashes—intervening darkness longer than light	Fl R 10 secs.
An occulting light	Appears as a steady beam broken by a short period of darkness	Occ.
An alternating light	Two to more colours in succession. You may have alternating flashing or alternating occulting	Alt. Fl or Alt. Occ.
Group flashing	Shows a regular group of flashes and intervening period of darkness	Gp Fl (4) R 15 secs.
Group occulting	Shows a steady beam broken by regular group of eclipses	G. occ. (3) 10 secs.
A fixed light	A steady beam	F.
Quick flashing	Continuous rapid flashes	Qk. A.

If colour is not indicated it is white, otherwise R=red, G=green. The light symbol is on top of the symbol for the buoy. E.g. Gp Fl (4) R 15 secs.=4 regular flashes in a group with a long period in between 15 secs. from first flash to first in next group—red colour.

What you do is to identify the light you see on the chart, note the type of buoy, and act accordingly.

Things to do and questions to answer

Chapters 1 and 2

1 Visit a harbour and look at all the things you see there in the light of what you have read in this chapter. Make a sketch map or plan of the harbour, and look at an Admiralty Chart to see how the harbour is shown on it. Talk to the Harbourmaster, and try to get a copy of the Byelaws of the Harbour Commissioners, or the Regulations of the Shipyards with regard to their moorings. Make drawings of the types of boats you see, and some anchors that can be seen at low water.

2 Make sketches of the types of boats you see in the dinghy park, and a typical rowing dinghy you may see on the hard, and label the parts you know, using the terms used to describe the hull in Chapter 1.

3 Make wall-charts to show:
(a) Positions in a boat.
(b) Directions and positions outside a boat.

4 (a) What is meant when a boat is said to be 'in commission'?
(b) What is a 'dinghy park', a 'fairway', and a 'hard'?

5 Recommend a type of anchor and its weight for general use in a 14 foot sailing boat. What size and length of anchor rope would you use?

6 Explain the meaning of the terms 'ground chain', 'riding scope', and 'mooring buoy'. Who is responsible for putting down moorings in a harbour?

7 Explain how an anchor works. Illustrate your answer.

8 What are the advantages of using a mooring?

9 Describe how to use an anchor.

Chapter 3

1 In your scrapbook or notebook draw all the types of sailing craft described in this chapter, and label them with titles and points of interest. Colour the sail plans to emphasize the differences.

2 Collect press or magazine cuttings of good examples of the various types of Rig, and paste them in your notebook.

3 Take photographs of craft under sail, and identify them according to type. When visiting an anchorage or sailing waters, you can always 'SPOT' the various type of craft, and this is often possible even when they are not actually under sail.

4 Make a wall-chart to illustrate how sailing boats are classified according to 'Rig'.

5 Draw: (*a*) a Bermudan Cutter, and (*b*) a Gaff Yawl, under full sail.

6 What is (*a*) a Headsail, (*b*) a Foresail, and (*c*) a Jib? What is a Staysail, and why is it so named?

7 (*a*) Explain the difference between a Ketch and a Yawl, and illustrate your answer.
(*b*) Explain the difference between a Bermudan Schooner and a Ship, and illustrate your answer.

8 (*a*) What are spars?
(*b*) What work is done by a gaff or a yard?
(*c*) What is the difference between a gaff and a yard?
(*d*) Name the spar at the foot of a sail.

9 Describe and draw: (*a*) a Genoa, (*b*) a Spinnaker.
What purpose do they serve?

10 Name the sails you find on a fully rigged Thames Barge, and illustrate your answer with a diagram.

Chapter 4

1 Collect press and magazine cuttings to illustrate what you now know about the different shapes of a boat's hull.

2 Make a wall-chart to illustrate the different shapes of bows and sterns about which you have read in this chapter.

3 Make models of sailing craft of days gone by, and the present time, giving special attention to the shape of the hull.

4 If possible visit a shipyard and see how hulls in various stages of assembly are built, and notice particularly how the various parts go together.

5 Draw sections of a boat's hull to show what is meant by round bilge, hard chine, multiple chine, clinker build, and a flattie.

6 Explain and illustrate what is meant by carvel-built, caulking, and strip planking.

7 Describe some of the ways in which a hull's shape affects its performance, and behaviour in the water.

8 What do you understand by 'draught', L W L, the beam-length ratio, reverse sheer, and deep keel?

9 Make a list of the materials from which a boat's hull may be made.

Chapter 5

1 Make drawings of: (a) Mainsails, and (b) Headsails, to illustrate how the various methods of cutting the cloths and sewing them together may be applied to these sails.

2 Search the magazines you have available for pictures of the different types of 'cut'. Label them and add them to your notebook.

3 If possible arrange a visit to a sailmaker's loft and see the processes by which sails are made, and the materials used.

4 Collect samples of the materials from which sails are made. Label them and mount them on a display board.

5 Draw: (a) a Bermudan mainsail, (b) a Gaff mainsail, and (c) a Headsail, and label as many parts and details as you can.

6 What is a 'bolt rope'? Where is it positioned, and why?

7 What is meant by 'bending a sail', 'shaking out a reef', and 'trimming your sails'?

8 Explain and illustrate what is meant by a cringle; a luff groove; mast track; batten pockets; and a headboard.

9 Describe what is meant by 'shape' in a sail, and how it is obtained or produced in the making of a sail.

10 What kind of rope is recommended as best for use as bolt rope with cotton sails? Give the formula for calculating its breaking strain and working load. What is the working load of 2-inch rope of this material?

11 Draw to the scale of 1 inch to 4 feet each of the following:

(a) A Bermudan mainsail measuring 12 feet on the foot, and 26 feet on the luff. The roach is 1 foot wide at its mid point.
(b) A Gaff mainsail measuring 14 feet on the foot, 12 feet on the luff, with a head of 10 feet and leech of 16 feet. (N.B. Use a pair of compasses to find the intersection of the head and the leech, and assume an angle of 90 degrees at the tack.)
(c) A Headsail with a 15 feet luff, foot of 6 feet and leech 13 feet.

12 Calculate the 'measured' area of each sail mentioned in Question 11. Note that the 'measured' area ignores the curvature in the shape of the sail, and the roach is discounted too, it being regarded as 'free' area. Make any additional measurements required from the scale drawings.

Chapter 6

1　Make a number of models to illustrate the different patterns of Standing Rigging. (Flat hulls about 1 foot long are recommended, and the rigging can be of thin wire or waxed whipping twine tied to small screw-eyes.)

2　Make a larger model to show both Standing and Running Rigging of any particular boat in which you are likely to sail a good deal. (Again a simple flat hull is recommended, about 2 feet long with the rest of the work scaled up from this. This should be a working model as far as the rigging and the fittings are concerned.)

3　Make models to illustrate 'mechanical aids' to work—pulley blocks and purchases, winch drums, levers. There may be models of this kind in a science laboratory to which you have access.

4　Explain the difference between Standing and Running Rigging, and describe the work of the latter.

5　How is a mast stayed? Illustrate your answer.

6　Show by drawings where you find the following, and explain the work of each: gooseneck, gaff jaws, mastbands, crosstrees, bottle-screws, and chain plates.

7　What is meant by: a fall of rope, a rope tail, to reeve a rope, to set up a backstay, to trim a sail?

8　Make a drawing to show the position of all the spars on a Gaff Yawl.

9　Show by means of diagrams the Standing Rigging you expect to support a 30 foot Bermudan mast.

10　Name two modern racing dinghies, and one older boat with no Standing Rigging.

11　Explain the work of: (*a*) a Topping Lift, and (*b*) a Kicking Strap.

12　Describe the items of Running Rigging required for setting and working a Gaff Mainsail.

13　Show by diagrams where you find the following on a sailing boat, and explain the work of each: a horse, a clawring, a winch, a jackstay and a bumkin. (All illustrated in diagrams.)

Chapter 7

1　Obtain (*a*) about four feet of 1-inch hemp, and finish the ends. Use this to make and learn the various knots, bends and hitches you wish to know; (*b*) about three feet of 1-inch hemp, and unlay the ends for about four inches, and whip each strand.

169

2 Use this to practice splicing.

3 Use short lengths of rope with the ends finished in the proper manner to make examples of all the knots, bends, hitches, and splices mentioned in this chapter. Mount each on a display board, with appropriate labels.

4 Note particularly which knots, bends, and hitches various skippers and their crews use in boatwork. With this information, and that contained in this chapter, make a summary for your own use, of 'the knot for the job'.

5 (a) What materials are used for making rope?
   (b) Draw a diagram to show how cordage is made, and label its parts clearly.

6 Name the different methods of finishing a rope's end, and describe and illustrate one of them in detail.

7 Name the different methods of stowing a rope, and describe and illustrate one of them.

8 Mention some of the differences between wire rope and cordage.

9 List six jobs required to be done by knots, bends, and hitches, and name one knot, bend or hitch you would recommend for each job.

10 Describe and illustrate how you would:
   (a) Belay a rope, and
   (b) Make and hang a Coil on a Cleat.

11 Say what you know about a Heaving Line.

12 Describe and illustrate how you would make either a Short Splice or a Long Splice. What advantage has the Long Splice?

13 What do you understand by Worming, Parcelling and Serving a rope?

14 Describe briefly how a rope is measured for length, size and strength.

Chapter 8

1 Watch boats under sail. Note what point of sailing they are on by the position of the sails, and the wind direction.

2 Make a model sailing yacht. Learn to manipulate it on the water. Watch the relationship between sail position and wind direction.

3 Look at pictures of sailing boats, and from them decide two things:
   (a) From where is the wind coming in relation to the boat, and
   (b) On what point of sailing is each boat?

4 Explain the difference between True and Apparent Wind in relation to a sailing boat.

5 Mention three things that the surrounding water does in relation to a sailing boat.

6 What are the three main 'points of sailing'? Draw a plan view of a lugsail dinghy marking the position of the mainsail for each point of sailing.

7 Explain and illustrate what is meant by the 'Orange Pip Theory' of how a boat sails.

8 On what point of sailing are each of the boats shown in the illustration below? State whether each boat is on Port or Starboard Tack.

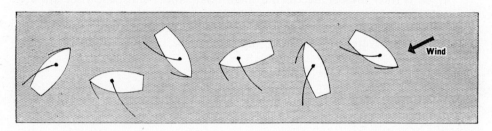

9 A boat is running with a wind of 7 knots dead astern, and is making 5 knots through the water. What is the speed of the apparent wind?

10 What do you know about the meaning of 'off the wind', 'on the wind', 'head to wind'?

11 (a) Each of the boats shown in the illustration below is sailing. Reproduce this drawing, and mark in the position of wind for each boat.
(b) On which tack is each boat?

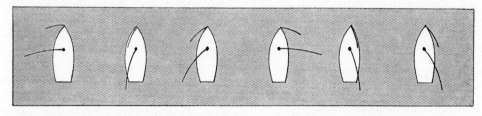

12 Reproduce the illustration opposite:

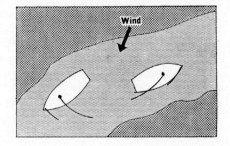

(a) Shade the windward side of the boat which has the wind aft.
(b) The wind backs 4 points (a point=$11\frac{1}{4}°$. 32 points in the 360° of the compass). Draw and label the new wind.
(c) Label the lee shore.
(d) On the boat which has the wind for'ard, mark in a line to show the beam.

171

Chapter 9

1 Observe the ebb and flow on a shore on several successive days, and note the 'tide line' (high water) left behind each day. Mark with a labelled pointer both high and low water over a period of a fortnight, and in this way you will improve your understanding of Spring and Neap Tides, and the other terms used to describe tides.

2 What do you understand by Spring and Neap Tides? How are they caused? What is their importance to the small boat sailor? Illustrate your answer.

3 What do you understand by the following terms as applied to tides—the flood, slack water, H W F and C, and taking off?

4 Describe how tides affect small boat sailors.

5 What units are used to measure: (a) speed, (b) the depth of water, and (c) distance at sea?

Chapter 10

1 On a postcard make a summary of the things you have to do in preparing a sailing boat to get under way. Memorize your postcard notes on this subject.

2 Watch what an experienced skipper and his crew do on launching a sailing boat, and in preparing to get under way from a mooring or off a shore.

3 Describe a typical yacht's tender and her equipment. Say what you know about going afloat in a rowing dinghy. Illustrate your answer.

4 What do you call:
   (a) The rope used to hoist a mainsail? If there is more than one, what are their separate names?
   (b) The flag used to indicate wind direction—what else may such a flag indicate?
   (c) The pieces of wood or plastic used to stiffen the sails?

5 What do you use to empty and dry out the bilges of your half-decked or open boat in which rain water has collected whilst lying on her mooring? Why do you carry out this work?

6 Find out details of three types of 'self baling' apparatus that have been developed to empty your boat of unwanted water, and which do this work when the boat is under way. Explain how each works, and illustrate your answer with simple diagrams.

7 Describe some of the difficulties that may arise if you leave your mooring and proceed to sea without:

(*a*) An anchor (properly secured).

(*b*) A baler (or water pump).

(*c*) A pair of oars (or paddles).

(*d*) Buoyancy Apparatus (not properly secured or uninflated).

(*e*) A Burgee or Racing Flag (as the case demands).

8 You leave your mooring sailing with the wind aft, and soon remember that the working of the centre-board has not been checked. It is then found to be jammed in the 'up' position and you fail to move it. How does this limit your sailing? What immediate action do you suggest, and how do you carry it out?

9 Explain how you would dress for sailing in rough weather in an estuary, and what points govern your choice of clothing.

Chapter 11

1 Make a set of diagrams to show in what order you hoist the sails in getting under way: (*a*) with the wind coming from for'ard, and (*b*) with the wind aft of the beam.

2 When watching from the shore, make a note of how various craft get under way under different conditions.

3 Go to an open Dinghy Meeting. Look at trolleys and how they are constructed; see how boats are launched, and how the helmsmen and crew get them away from a shore. Think of all you see in relation to what you have read in this chapter.

4 What factors influence the way boats lie at moorings or at anchor?

5 As you stand in your boat lying at anchor, the wind appears to come from right aft. Which sail do you hoist first to get under way in your Bermudan sloop? What action do you take to complete the manoeuvre?

6 What do the sails do when a boat is turned head to wind? What action do you take at the tiller to turn a boat into the wind? Assume you are sitting to windward at the helm.

7 In getting under way from an anchorage with the wind coming from ahead, why do you not hoist the jib first?

8 Explain the difficulties that arise in hoisting a mainsail with the wind aft.

9 What is a 'Sternboard'? Draw a diagram to show how this might be used to help getting under way from a crowded mooring.

10 Describe a simple method of getting a sailing dinghy away from a lee shore.

173

Chapter 12

1 Make postcard summaries about 'Boat Handling' for various situations and points of sailing. Pay particular attention to the action necessary to go from one point of sailing to the other and to turn your boat.

2 Practice handling a small boat on your own. Wear a life-jacket, get someone to watch you from the shore or bank, choose a fine day with a light breeze, and a slack tide, and use a stable 10- or 12-foot dinghy with one sail, i.e. Una rigged. Even if you haven't sailed before you should have some success. If the boat is much bigger, and is a sloop, and conditions are anything other than ideal, then do not venture out on your own without a competent person with you.

3 What do you know about the normal situation or position of the centre-board for: (a) Beating; (b) Reaching; (c) Running?

4 What do you understand by trimming a boat? Explain boat trim in relation to the various points of sailing.

5 How do you check the trim of the sails:
(a) when sailing close hauled, and
(b) when reaching?

6 How do you turn a sailing boat at the end of a tack?
Explain the terms 'in stays' and 'in irons'.

7 Explain the work of: (a) a helmsman, and (b) the crew in a sailing boat.

8 What do you understand by: (a) an accidental gybe, and (b) broaching to? What precautions may you take to avoid each?

9 Describe how you would execute a controlled gybe.

10 How do you deal with:
(a) an unexpected gust when beating to windward;
(b) excessive rolling when running with the wind aft;
(c) overpowering weather helm when reaching fast;
(d) a boat that is sluggish in stays, and tends not to come about?

11 Describe the principles to be observed when picking up moorings or anchoring.

12 Describe what measures you take when stowing ship.

Chapter 13

1 Try to visit a museum, an institute, or a research establishment that has an 'air tunnel' and see a model sail being tested.

2 In what way does the wind transfer its motive power to a sailing boat?

3 Explain in what way a sail is different from an aeroplane wing.

4 What features would you look for in a sailing boat that help to improve the airflow past the mainsail?

5 Say what you know about: (*a*) Heeling, and (*b*) the Work of the Centre-board in a small sailing boat.

6 What do you understand by 'Lee Helm'? In what way is it dangerous? What is its cause? What measures would you try to cure Lee Helm?

7 What do you understand by 'Helm Balance'? Make a list of the features that contribute towards this.

Chapter 14

1 Detail all the things the helmsman has to do when gybing deliberately.

2 Where would you recommend a helmsman to sit when running goose-winged? Give your reasons.

3 How do you reduce rolling when running before the wind? If this fails, what is the remedy?

4 Draw a boat with her spinnaker set. Label the ropes that control the sail and explain their work.

5 How would you equip your boat specially for sailing in light airs?

6 (*a*) When roller reefing how do you prevent the boom from drooping? Illustrate.
(*b*) What danger must you guard against when hoisting sail after shaking out a reef tied with reef pendants?

7 Describe how you pick up one of your crew who has fallen overboard. Illustrate your answer.

8 On what point of sailing would you take way off your boat to make some temporary adjustment?

9 Write an essay on 'Sailing your boat well and safety precautions in heavy weather'.

10 Describe the most certain method of getting off a lee shore after your boat has touched the bottom.

Chapter 15

1 Make a list of the Do's and Dont's of handling your boat carefully so as to reduce wear and tear.

2 Keep a log of your boat's sailing hours, an inventory and a record of work done on her, and outstanding items needing attention from week to week.

3 Make a tabulated list of things to be looked at and inspected at the laying up and fitting out of your boat.

4 Why is it worth looking after your boat carefully?

5 When is this work likely to be done?

6 What does looking after your boat involve?

7 What are the important points in your day to day care of the sails?

8 Describe how you would 'stretch' your new cotton sails. How do sails made from synthetic fibres differ in this respect?

9 What is the purpose of anti-fouling paint, and how is it applied?

10 Explain how you would refit a hull the paintwork of which is badly flaked and bubbling.

11 What conditions are necessary to produce good varnish work?

12 What do you look for when inspecting cordage? How do you maintain your cordage in the best possible condition?

13 What new materials have been introduced for the construction of hull, rigging and sails that alter the whole scheme of caring for your boat?

Chapter 16

1 Make a set of models of both sailing and power craft with which you can practise the rule of the road at sea. You need three sailing boats and three power craft. They need be no larger than six inches overall length, and in the case of the sailing boats, the sail position should be easy to adjust. You can use your models on any table, and arrange them to illustrate various situations, and show the action to be taken. They can be used in this way to provide team games.

After reading the chapter on the Buoyage System, you may add to your collection, scale models of the various buoys in use. Whatever situations you then create with your sailing boats and power craft, may have added to them any navigational limits imposed by the Buoyage System.

2 Make a set of wall-charts to illustrate:
(a) the Rule of the Road under Sail, and
(b) the Steering Rules for Power Vessels.

3 What action is taken by a vessel that has right of way when being approached by one whose duty it is to keep clear?

4 Mention three power craft that have right of way over sailing boats because they are 'hampered' vessels* (i.e. they are less manoeuvrable).

* Such vessels are sometimes described as being 'not under command'.

5 What should a sailing vessel use to give sound signals?
What is the duration of a short blast?

6 What sound signals do vessels give to indicate they are altering course?
What is the most important consideration before such signals are given?

7 Comment on the decision of a skipper who orders 'full speed ahead so that we can cross ahead of that vessel on our starboard bow'. Quote the two vital rules to support your comment.

8 Does a large sailing vessel running with the wind aft, have to keep clear of a fleet of small sailing dinghies she is overtaking? Quote the rule as given in this chapter. Does this also apply under the proposed new rules of 1960?

9 Quote either:
(a) The Right of Way Section of the Royal Yacht Association Racing Rules of 1960, OR
(b) Articles 17, 20, and 24 of the proposed new rules for the Prevention of Collisions at Sea 1960.
Are there any differences between these two sets of rules?

Chapter 17

1 Add lights to any models you made for Chapter 16, Rule of the Road, Question 1. All your problems may now be re-enacted for conditions during the hours of darkness.

2 Make wall-charts to illustrate the lights carried by:
(a) Sailing vessels, and
(b) Power craft, and add to them the lights of any 'special vessels' operating in your area.

3 What are the lights called carried by vessels at anchor? Describe their position, colour and arc of visibility.

4 What is the difference between being 'under way', and 'making way'? What is understood by being 'not under command'? How does a disabled vessel show this by night?

5 Draw a plan view to show the lights carried by:
(a) a power vessel under 40 tons;
(b) a sailing vessel over 20 tons.

6 (a) What are the three main positions in which a vessel carries her lights?
(b) What colour do you associate with each of these positions under normal conditions under way by night?
(c) What arc of visibility do you associate with these positions?

7 What sound signals do you give in a sailing vessel in thick weather? What sound signals do you hear from a steam vessel in thick weather? Mention any other useful sound signals you may give in thick weather.

177

8 During what hours must all lights mentioned in the Rules be shown?

9 What lights may a sailing vessel of under 20 tons carry instead of those laid down for a larger vessel? What light must a rowing boat carry when under oars or sail?

10 Mention some of the types of vessels that carry lights different from normal. Why do they require to do this?

Chapter 18

1 Prepare a wall-chart to show the shape and colour of:
(*a*) Port and Starboard Hand Buoys;
(*b*) Wreck Buoys;
(*c*) Mid-channel Buoys;
(*d*) Middle Ground Buoys;
(*e*) Buoys with a special purpose.
At this stage omit Topmarks and Lights.

2 If you sail or live in a locality where the waters are buoyed, and other marks exist like beacons, lighthouses or light vessels, obtain a chart to show the area (either an Admiralty Chart or a Stanford's Coloured Chart for Coastal Navigators). Make a practice copy of this chart, taking off only the shore outline, the buoyage system, and showing the shoals and navigable channels. This exercise will give you a useful wall-chart. Explore the area in a sailing or rowing dinghy, and locate on the water the buoys or other sea marks that you have marked on the chart. In this way you learn thoroughly the buoyage in your particular area. Unless completely unavoidable, never sail in strange waters without making yourself familiar with the buoyage system. (At least on the chart.)

3 Make notes and drawings of the Topmarks that exist in your particular area, and what they mean in relation to the buoys that carry them.

4 When you are familiar with the buoyage system as it appears during daylight, make notes on what lights appear on the buoys during the hours of darkness. Add a flash of the *correct* colour and the abbreviated symbols to show the character of the light in each case. Do this on the wall-chart you prepared earlier, showing your particular area.

5 Explain briefly the difference between a map and a chart. Mention some of the items found on a chart that are useful to sailors.

6 What are buoys, and what work do they do? Why need you study the buoyage system?

7 How do you read or interpret the buoyage system? Explain the meaning of Port Hand and Starboard Hand in relation to this. Draw and colour port and starboard hand buoys.

8 What is the work of a mid-channel buoy? Draw and colour two different mid-channel buoys. On which side do you pass a mid-channel buoy? Give the reason for your answer.

9 On which side do you pass a starboard hand buoy when going seaward from an estuary?

10 Draw, colour and mark the various kinds of wreck buoy. Mention two other ways of indicating a wreck. How do you know on which side a wreck should be passed?

11 What is the work of a middle ground buoy? Describe the shape and colour of middle ground buoys. What is the significance of the colour?

12 Name the work and distinguishing colour of any three buoys used for a special purpose.

13 How may buoys be distinguished by night? Explain what you know about this system of lighted buoys.

Appendix

Recommendations of the International Conference on
SAFETY OF LIFE AT SEA - 1960
Regulations for the prevention of collisions at sea

The appropriate committee has been asked to forward these revised regulations to the Governments concerned, and when unanimity has been reached as to their acceptance, to fix a date on and after which they shall apply. They will supplant the rules (1–4) under the paragraph heading 'Rules of the Road under Sail' in Chapter 16 of this book.

Rule 17

(a) When two sailing vessels are approaching one another, so as to involve risk of collision, one of them shall keep out of the way of the other as follows:

(i) When each has the wind on a different side, the vessel which has the wind on the port side shall keep out of the way of the other.

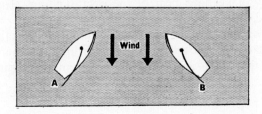

(ii) When both have the wind on the same side, the vessel which is to windward shall keep out of the way of the vessel which is to leeward.

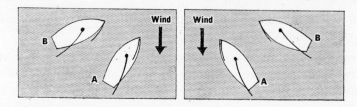

(b) For the purposes of this Rule the windward side shall be deemed to be the side opposite to that on which the mainsail is carried or, in the case of a square-rigged vessel, the side opposite to that on which the largest fore-and-aft sail is carried.

Rule 20

(a) When a power-driven vessel and a sailing vessel are proceeding in such directions as to involve risk of collision, except as provided for in Rules 24 and 26, the power-driven vessel shall keep out of the way of the sailing vessel.

(b) This Rule shall not give to a sailing vessel the right to hamper, in a narrow channel, the safe passage of a power-driven vessel which can navigate only inside such channel.

(c) A seaplane on the water shall, in general, keep well clear of all vessels and avoid impeding their navigation. In circumstances, however, where risk of collision exists, she shall comply with these Rules.

Rule 24

(a) Notwithstanding anything contained in these Rules, every vessel overtaking any other shall keep out of the way of the overtaken vessel.

(b) Every vessel coming up with another vessel from any direction more than $22\frac{1}{2}$ degrees (2 points) abaft her beam, i.e. in such a position, with reference to the vessel which she is overtaking, that at night she would be unable to see either of that vessel's sidelights, shall be deemed to be an overtaking vessel; and no subsequent alteration of the bearing between the two vessels shall make the overtaking vessel a crossing vessel within the meaning of these Rules, or relieve her of the duty of keeping clear of the overtaken vessel until she is finally past and clear.

(c) If the overtaking vessel cannot determine with certainty whether she is forward of or abaft this direction from the other vessel, she shall assume that she is an overtaking vessel and keep out of the way.

Glossary

This Glossary does not include any terms the meaning of which is already made clear in the text

ALL STANDING	unexpectedly or suddenly and with sails still set
AWASH	level with the water
BARE POLES	a sailing boat under bare poles is under way but with no sail set
BEAM ENDS	a boat on her beam ends is one right over resting on her topsides
BOOT TOPPING	the painted band or strip near the water-line of a boat and reaching from stem to stern between the bottom and topsides
BRIGHTWORK	generally varnished woodwork or polished metal fittings
BULL'S-EYE	a round thimble made of hardwood
BUTT END	the largest end of any spar
CAPFUL OF WIND	just enough wind to fill the sails on a calm day
TO CARRY AWAY	to break away, e.g. to carry away a mast in a storm
CATSPAW	a light puff of wind on a calm day
TO COME UP WITH	to overtake another boat
CUDDY	originally the skipper's cabin—now commonly a small cabin on a small yacht
CUT WATER	a boat's stem
DEAD-EYE	a block of hardwood with a hole through which to reeve a rope; a fairlead or early form of block
DODGER	a canvas screen to protect against wind and spray
TO DRAG	to pull along an anchor or mooring in heavy weather
TO DRAW	describing the depth of a boat in the water—'she draws three feet'
EASY	haul or slack away carefully or slowly
FLEET	shallow or narrow coastal waters
TO FURL	to roll up
GRAPNEL	a small boat's anchor with three or four arms
GROUND SWELL	long smooth waves caused by a distant storm
HALF TIDE	e.g. a half tide rock, a half tide wreck; one that uncovers at half tide
HULK	a ship or boat hull unfit to use
JURY	temporary, e.g. jury-rig, jury-mast, etc
KILLICK	a small anchor (usually home-made)

181

LEEBOARD	a board fixed to the side of a vessel that can be lowered to serve the same purpose as a centre-board
LEE TIDE	a tide going to leeward
TO LET FLY	to let go at once—e.g. let fly the jibsheet
LIFE-LINES	rope rigged aboard on deck and often made fast to crew in heavy weather
MARTINGALE	like a bobstay—any stay that prevents a boom or spar from topping up; usually fitted under a jib-boom
NEAPED	a boat grounded until the next spring tides or that cannot leave an anchorage except at springs
TO PAY OFF	to fall away from the wind—to bear away
TO PAY OUT	to ease a rope by hand
A PREVENTER	an additional or stay rope fitted anywhere to stop a fitting or spar from moving
PUDDING	a rope fender
TO RAKE	to lean from the upright position
ROGUE'S YARN	a coloured thread in a rope strand—to distinguish different types of rope
SCANDALIZE	to lower a gaff or top boom in order to spill wind
SCANTLINGS	the sizes of the member parts used in a boat's structure
SHIPSHAPE	seamanship-like appearance
SPINDRIFT	spray from the tops of waves
TO START	to loosen, e.g. to start a plank, to start a rope
TO STAVE IN	to break a hole in a plank
TO SWEAT UP	to give an extra heave to a rope such as a halyard
TENDER	a small boat used for ferrying—a descriptive word for a boat that heels easily or is a crank—opposite from stiff
UNSTABLE	a boat that is tender or top-heavy
WASH	the disturbed water aft of a moving boat
WEATHER TIDE	a tide moving to windward
TO WEEP	to leak slightly

Index